☑ **W9-DBS-154**

Managing Young Adult Services

A Self-Help Manual

Renée J. Vaillancourt

Neal-Schuman Publishers, Inc.
New York   London

Published by Neal-Schuman Publishers, Inc.
100 Varick Street
New York, NY 10013

The paper used in this publication meets the minimum requirements of American National Standard for Information Sciences—Permanence of Paper for Printed Library Materials, ANSI Z39.48–1992. ∞

ISBN 1-55570-434-4

Contents

List of Figures

Series Editor Foreword

by Joel Shoemaker

- Have you started a new job working with teens in a school or public library and are not sure what your priorities should be?
- Were you trained and hired primarily to serve children, reference, or generalist duties and find yourself being handed young adult responsibilities as well?
- Are you working as a young adult librarian and wondering if you are focusing on the right things?
- Are you frustrated by roadblocks and are searching for solutions?
- Are you a veteran librarian, library media specialist, or teacher/librarian looking for fresh approaches to manage the day-to-day and year-in-year-out tasks of serving young adults?

Managing Young Adult Services: A Self-Help Manual, the newest book in the *teens @ the library series*, by Renée J. Vaillancourt, is geared toward answering these kinds of questions and more. Renée brings her years of practical experience as a young adult librarian, trainer, and consultant to provide practical and innovative solutions to specific situations that almost all librarians working with teens face at one time or another. She brings a fresh, interesting perspective and presents it in an easy-to-read, easy-to-use format.

Renée addresses the issues that she knows from both personal and professional experience can profoundly affect the delivery of the best possible services to young adults. Recognizing that young adults are in some ways unique from other patron groups and necessarily require some unique approaches, she suggests proven strategies for addressing the opportunities and challenges teens present.

Like all books in the *teens @ the library series*, *Managing Young Adult Services: A Self-Help Manual*, seeks to:

- Draw from the best, most current research
- Target the changing needs of today's teenagers
- Cite the most innovative models
- Provide practical suggestions that have been real-world tested
- Call on each of us to aim high

In that spirit I heartily recommend this book not only for those who feel they are novices in the field, but as a gut-check for those with experience who recognize that values, priorities, and personal goals are actually critical components of every aspect of management. Renée sagely reminds us that to provide good service to others we must first manage ourselves.

Foreword

by Patrick Jones

Young Adult librarians put on stellar programs, design teen Web pages, and develop diverse collections for a savvy audience. These collections, programs, and the rest of our services are successful because Young Adult librarians take risks, turn over collections, and respond to trends. Those are the things that our teen customers see. But what goes on before they enter the door? The planning, the communicating, the training, the leading, the mentoring and coaching, and the THINKING provide the foundation to make those things happen—not just today, but for all the Young Adult librarians, and young adults, who will work in and use our libraries for generations to come. The tools YA librarians use to provide this crucial infrastructure are management skills.

If you embrace Renée's concept that all Young Adult librarians are managers regardless of their titles, then you know that your real legacy isn't the collection you built, but the teenagers you served, the volunteers you inspired, the teen council members you empowered, and the staff you mentored. If you motivate one teen customer, volunteer, or shelver to enter the library profession, your legacy will live on in people and ideas, not in programs and books. If you develop a strategic plan of service; network in the community and within the library; design a Young Adult area for a new or renovated building; if you think big picture, you can cast a big shadow. If you leave the day-to-day work of Young Adult or school librarianship to move into higher management or school administration, then your big shadow casts an even wider net.

In this book, Renée has given Young Adult and school librarians the tools they need to develop, and then flex their management muscles. She doesn't just talk about time management, but provides lists, personal anecdotes, and ample sidebar quotes from management gurus to help readers practice it. Drawing on her work managing hordes of teen volunteers to that of a library administrator, she combines her practical experience with sound advice. But what is best about this book is how Renée has reached out of the field of librarianship into the arena of management, citing authors like Steven Covey and Peter Drucker, and integrating business management principles into the day-to-day work of managing teen services.

The successful approach to serving young adults in libraries involves realizing that Young Adult services is more than the latest award-winning novel or hot series, more than popular programs or information literacy activities. Successful Young Adult services are built around the holistic way in which teens use libraries. It places teens at the center and looks at how all parts of the library can play a role in meeting the unique needs of young adult patrons. In the same way, Renée has placed management of Young Adult services in the center. Young Adult services managers do everything that managers in libraries do: from the nuts and bolts of budgeting to the art of leadership. And although the Young Adult librarian may not be directly responsible for staff supervision, it is through the force of her conviction, personality, and leadership that services to teens can be transformed into the centerpiece of any library.

In the Preface, Renée notes "many public libraries still offer Young Adult services as an afterthought." If Young Adult librarians follow her advice and position themselves as managers, leaders, and mentors, then directors and library boards will have to realize the benefits of serving young adults. What Young Adult librarians do is present teen customers with opportunities. Through the services that Young Adult librarians plan, develop, implement, and evaluate, teen customers are provided with an abundance of choices which will lead to lifelong learning and healthy youth development. That's the real work of librarians working with teens: supporting teens' successful transformation through adolescence with a holistic service response. Young Adult librarians help teenagers unlock their potential. By unlocking our own potential as managers and leaders, we can demonstrate not only our worth, but the value of teenagers in libraries and in society.

Preface

Managing Young Adult Services: A Self-Help Manual addresses the many challenges facing YA librarians. Working with teenagers can bring out the best and the worst in all of us. On the one hand, they inspire us with their energy, their idealism, and their creativity and commitment to causes they believe in. Observing their rapid growth and continual process of self-exploration causes us to constantly learn, and question our own assumptions. On the other hand, young adults can be fiercely judgmental (of themselves and others) and are often subject to mood extremes that can be trying even to the most caring and patient adults (not to mention the kids themselves!). Teens can be loud and excitable, and are sometimes involved in so many activities that it's hard for them to follow through on commitments that they make with the best of intentions.

Add to this the fact that many public libraries still offer Young Adult services as an afterthought (if they offer targeted services to teens at all, rather than grouping adolescents under the umbrella of Youth Services), and poorer schools sometimes can't provide professional librarians at all. Then consider the all-too-common tendency for librarians to spend hours of their personal time, and dollars from their often meager salaries, to try and make up for the inadequacies of the system. Often YA and school library budgets and staffing are inadequate to serve this ever-increasing segment of the population. Put all of these factors together and you have a sure-fire recipe for burnout.

SO WHAT'S A LIBRARIAN TO DO?

In *Managing Young Adult Services*, I have attempted to provide management principles and strategies that should work equally well for school or public librarians serving young adults. In an age where there is increasing overlap between personal and work time, I also provide some general self-help principles (like developing organizational skills and learning stress-reduction techniques) that librarians can apply to their personal as well as their professional lives.

The book is divided into two parts, which I refer to as Leadership and Administration. Chapters One through Four in the Leadership section provide most of the interpersonal strategies that many people think of when they think about management. Chapters Five through Ten in the Administration section address more practical task-management skills as well as strategies for effective self-management.

Chapter One provides an overview of basic relational principles that can be applied to anyone, be they staff, colleagues, bosses, or young adults. Suggestions are also provided for improving communications skills, which I believe is the heart of effective management. This chapter explains what it means to be a coach, and also provides suggestions for troubleshooting problems. It concludes with an examination of common issues related to leadership and supervision.

The second chapter addresses the management challenges in working directly with young adults. It begins with a consideration of how teens and adults are different, and what we have in common. Information about adolescent development, teen stressors, and young adult trends are provided to help us better understand our primary patrons. This chapter concludes with a discussion of various ways to interact with young adults, and how to provide fair and effective discipline when necessary.

Chapter Three discusses the issues involved in supervising other library workers, be they staff members, teachers, or volunteers. It begins with tips on hiring and training new YA staff, and continues to discuss the importance of personal accountability and teamwork. Suggestions on running effective meetings and providing staff evaluations are provided, and the chapter concludes with information about how to express appreciation and address problems with library workers.

Chapter Four focuses on an area that is not often considered when discussing management: the importance of managing relationships with bosses and colleagues. It also provides strategies for effective networking within your community on the local, regional, state, and national levels, and concludes with a discussion of the role of youth advocacy in a young adult or school librarian's job.

Part Two of *Managing Young Adult Services: A Self-Help Manual* begins with Chapter Five. It provides information about managing Young Adult or school library collections, resources (including technology), programs and events. A step-by-step guide for planning a program with an outside speaker or performer, and helpful resources for information on author visits are also provided.

Chapter Six addresses the "P" words: paperwork and planning. Though many librarians dread these tasks, they are the foundation of effective Young Adult services. The YA planning process includes determining standards of service for staff, and roles and service responses for the department. Librarians will learn how to create mission, vision, and values statements for Young Adult or school library services with the help of teens. Goals and objectives will follow from these statements of purpose and policies and procedures will be put in place to achieve those goals. Reports and statistics are used to measure progress, and a formal evaluation of services completes the process.

Chapter Seven teaches Young Adult or school librarians how to get, manage, and spend money wisely. It provides strategies to increase your Young Adult budget through a reallocation of funds in the library or from outside funding. The importance of creating and maintaining a Young Adult budget is discussed, and tips on record-keeping are offered. The chapter concludes with suggestions on how to evaluate whether your money is being spent in the most effective ways.

In Chapter Eight, librarians will learn how to figure out where their time goes, where their time should be going, and how to adjust their schedules to focus on those priorities. Organizational tips are also offered in the interest of avoiding time-wasting activities that result from disorganization.

Many Young Adult and school librarians often feel overwhelmed by the immensity and importance of the work that they do. Chapter Nine will offer tips on managing stress that include meditation, mindfulness, eating well, and exercising. It will also provide strategies for addressing stressful feelings when they occur and information about when to get professional help.

Chapter Ten focuses on the librarian as an individual and how our personal lives inevitably affect our professional lives. Strategies are provided to become the manager of your own life by determining personal priorities, creating a personal mission statement, and achieving life goals. Suggestions on how to balance home and work responsibilities are also included.

Please note that throughout the book I have used the pronoun "she" to refer to librarians. Seventy-nine percent of public librarians are women and I suspect that those figures may be higher in youth services and school libraries. I have used the terms "teens," "young adults," and, in some cases, "kids" to refer to people between the ages of 12 to 18. While some librarians consider the term "kids" to be pejorative, most teens that I know call themselves kids, and would prefer that adults (including librarians) would call them "kids" rather than "young adults." In no way do I mean this term to confuse the important distinction between children and teenagers, or the services that are provided to them in libraries.

HOW WILL BUSINESS AND MANAGEMENT TECHNIQUES MAKE YOUR LIFE EASIER?

Edwin "Sam" Clay, the director of the Fairfax County (Virginia) Library System (and an instructor at Catholic University's School of Library and Information Science), maintains that library directors would be better off getting an MBA rather than an MLS. When I was in library school, he taught a class called "Management Principles," in which he required us to create our own management philosophy. At the time I thought this was a waste of time, since I never intended to become a library director, or even an assistant director or branch manager. I wanted to work with kids.

Over the years, as I worked as a children's librarian, a Young Adult librarian, and eventually a Young Adult services department coordinator, I began to see how the management principles that I learned in this class (which, incidentally, used such non-traditional texts as Sun Tsu's *The Art of War* and Deborah Tannen's *You Just Don't Understand*) applied to all aspects of librarianship, as well as to life in general.

Eventually, I did wind up moving into public library management. (I now believe that libraries need youth advocates at all levels.) As the assistant director of the Missoula (Mont.) Public Library in 1998–2000, I began to read business resources and attend management seminars that presented theories and techniques that would have been very useful for me to know when I was working directly with YAs. My intent, in this book, is not to invent new management techniques, but rather to apply tried-and-true business theories and management principles to libraries and to adapt library management philosophies to Young Adult services in particular.

HOW IS A YOUNG ADULT LIBRARIAN A MANAGER?

Many Young Adult librarians don't consider themselves to be managers because they don't have responsibility for supervising staff members. In the same way that all mothers are working mothers, I believe that all librarians are managers. We all manage resources, money, projects, events, and time. Young Adult librarians, by definition, manage young adults, and we often also supervise volunteers and student workers, if not traditional staff members. School library media specialists manage students, teachers, and parents. And we all do our best to manage stress and to find balance between our work and personal lives.

Each chapter of *Managing Young Adult Services* addresses one of these themes, and they can be read independently, for suggestions on particular topics, or consecutively for a more holistic approach. Although this book is intended specifically for Young Adult librarians in public libraries to school library media specialists, it may also appeal to library generalists, or administrators who are interested in simplifying, organizing, reducing stress, and better managing their lives and careers.

Acknowledgments

As with all publications in the library field, this book is a collaboration. I am grateful to all of the practicing librarians who provided me with ideas and information about how they manage Young Adult services. I am also grateful to those librarians who have written their own books and articles that were cited in this book. The authors and publishers of business management and self-help books were also incredibly generous in allowing me to reprint excerpts from their works.

Joel Shoemaker, who invited me to contribute to this series, has been an editor, source of information, and cheerleader through the whole process. Charles Harmon and Michael Kelley of Neal-Schuman answered countless questions and provided helpful editorial advice. Gary Albert shepharded the book throughout production and Arlene Quaratiello created the index. I would also like to thank the copyeditors, proofreaders, typesetters, and other behind-the-scenes people who helped to make this book a reality. I am grateful to Patrick Jones for writing the Foreword (and for his leadership in the field of Young Adult services and consistent encouragement and support of my work).

Pam Barry, Sam Clay, and Bette Ammon are managers that I look up to and have learned a lot from. Patrick Hogan provided me with several leads on appropriate topics and management gurus. My mother, Mary Vaillancourt, taught me all that I know about organization and time management. My father, Raymond Vaillancourt, taught me how to manage stress. My brother, Christien Vaillancourt, just wants his name mentioned in the acknowledgments (his son, Camron, is the cutest baby ever). And my husband, Sean McGrath, tolerated an out-of-balance work/life situation while I was writing this book. I am deeply grateful for his patience and support of my personal and professional development.

Part I

Leadership

Chapter 1

Basic Management Principles

BUILDING RELATIONSHIPS

Most of the basic principles of being a good manager boil down to being a good people-person. This will come more naturally to some people than to others, but everyone is capable of improving her social skills. This means learning how to communicate clearly and be a careful listener. It also means forming relationships with your subordinates that result in mutual trust and understanding. Here are some techniques to help you develop these skills.

Myers-Briggs—To Help Understand Yourself and Others

The Myers-Briggs model of personality type was developed in the 1940s by Katharine Briggs and her daughter, Isabel Briggs Myers, who based their work on Carl Jung's model of psychological types (Tieger and Barron-Tieger, 1992: 10–11). It differs from many other personality instruments (such as the Enneagram) in that it measures personality preferences on a number of levels, which provides a more comprehensive portrait of an individual. The Myers-Briggs model uses four personality preference scales to categorize people into 16 distinct personality types. Understanding these types can give a manager great insights into the preferences and motivations of her staff members, and herself!

Personality type can be determined by using the Myers-Briggs Type Indicator® (MBTI®) that is available through Consulting Psychologists Press (www.cpp-db.com), and administered by a trained professional, or on a more informal basis through questionnaires that are widely available on the Web and in print. "The aim of the MBTI is to identify, from self-report of easily recognized reactions, the basic preferences of people in regard to perception and judgement, so that the effects of each pref-

3

What We All Have in Common
While the Myers-Briggs model helps us to understand each other's differences, Phillip McGraw suggests that it is also useful to keep in mind our similarities. He maintains that we all share the following ten common characteristics:

1. The number-one fear among all people is rejection.
2. The number-one need among all people is acceptance.
3. To manage people effectively, you must do it in a way that protects or enhances their self-esteem.
4. Everybody—and I mean everybody—approaches every situation with at least some concern about "what's in it for me?"
5. Everybody—and I mean everybody—prefers to talk about things that are important to them personally.
6. People hear and incorporate only what they understand.
7. People like, trust, and believe those who like them.
8. People often do things for other than the apparent reasons.
9. Even people of quality can be, and often are, petty and small.
10. Everybody—and I mean everybody—wears a social mask. You must look beyond the mask to see the person. (McGraw, 1999: 49–50)

McGraw, Phillip © 1999. *Life Strategies: Doing What Works, Doing What Matters.* New York: Hyperion: 49–50.

erence, singly and in combination, can be established by research and put to practical use" (Myers and McCaulley, 1985:1). The MBTI is the most widely-used instrument to determine individual personality variations.

The Myers-Briggs Type Indicator can be used in situations requiring cooperation and teamwork and to enhance communication. Having a consultant do an in-service training on Myers-Briggs at the library is an excellent way to promote better understanding among all staff members. This would allow everyone in the department to learn each other's personality type and provide strategies to address communication and cooperation issues. A Young Adult services manager or school media specialist might even consider assigning work tasks according to personality preference (in consultation with the staff members involved, of course) to allow each staff member to maximize her strengths.

The ten characteristics that McGraw presents (see above) remind us that even those colleagues who may seem supremely self-confident are often vulnerable and concerned about being accepted. Often, when dealing with staff problems it is useful to keep in mind the basic human qualities inherent in each person and try to address comments to the person behind the mask.

Common Courtesy

As our lives become more hectic and stressful, we often forget to take time for the common courtesies we were taught by our parents and teachers in grade school. In her essay on "Establishing Staff Relations," Kathy Toon emphasizes the importance of being friendly with staff members and reminds managers to practice these simple habits:

> Greeting people with good morning or good afternoon
> Using please and thank you
> Giving staff your undivided attention
> Listening to what they say and not lecturing
> Avoiding sarcasm
> Apologizing if you are late or interrupt a meeting (1995: 146)

These are all basic tenets of customer service we use with our patrons daily. We must remember to apply these principles to our internal customers (our colleagues) as well.

Technology has made our lives easier in many ways, but it has also increased the number of things we are expected to get done in one day, and etiquette is often the first thing to get cut from the list. I have noticed that people often forget to say "thank you," to respond in a timely manner, or to acknowledge receipt of a message when communicating via e-mail. Although you may not be able to see the person you're corresponding with over the Internet, that person is still there and deserves the same kind of courtesy you would give to a person standing in front of you. This goes for staff members as well as patrons and colleagues.

Communication via e-mail often feels less formal than traditional correspondence, but it leaves the same paper trail. Defense Secretary Donald Rumsfeld advises his staff not to "do or say things you would not like to see on the front page of the *Washington Post*" (Robbins, 2001: A1, A6). Although it is much less likely for public or school librarians to find their words on the front page of the *Washington Post*, thoughtless discourtesies can come back to haunt us in similar ways. Remember that library e-mail is library property, and inappropriate messages (personal e-mail or criticisms of bosses or employees) on the library's e-mail system could result in lawsuits or disciplinary action.

The Emotional Bank Account

In *The 7 Habits of Highly Effective People*, Stephen Covey introduces the concept of an Emotional Bank Account. His theory is that people make deposits into the Emotional Bank Accounts of others by attending to the little things, keeping commitments, clarifying expectations, and showing personal integrity (1989: 192–197). Having a high balance in your Emotional Bank Account with someone allows you to make occasional withdrawals (mistakes) without destroying the relationship. However, if your Emotional Bank Account with someone is low, it will take very little to overdraw on the account. Therefore, to build a healthy Emotional Bank Account, it is essential to develop personal relationships with staff members—to learn what kinds of things are important to them and to express interest in these things.

James Kouzes and Barry Posner found that people most often define *credibility* as "doing what you say you will do." "This simple definition leads to a simple prescription for strengthening credibility: DWYSYWD—do what you say you will do. DWYSYWD has two essential parts: the first is 'say' and the second is 'do'" (Kouzes and Posner, 1993: 47).

This applies to deadlines as well as promises. If you say you are going to do something, do it. And if, for some reason, you can't, let the other person know *in advance* you won't be able to come through, and why. If at all possible, find a way to make it up to him (by mutually agreeing to an acceptable alternative) and apologize sincerely when you can't follow through on your commitment.

Everyone brings her own expectations to work situations, and often people subconsciously judge each other based on those expectations. Therefore, it is important to encourage the open sharing of expectations. This will insure that everyone is on the same page when you begin a project and will help to avoid misunderstandings down the line.

I define *integrity* as living in accordance with one's values, and I believe integrity is essential in order to be an effective manager. Covey defines integrity as "be[ing] loyal to those who are not present" (1989: 196). This means never saying anything about anyone that you wouldn't say

> Don't tolerate discourtesy [. . . .] One learns to be courteous—it is needed to enable different people who don't necessarily like each other to work together. Good causes do not excuse bad manners. Bad manners rub people raw; they do leave permanent scars. And good manners make a difference . . . . (Drucker, 1990: 114–115)

to his face. This is a very difficult principle to put into practice because a common form of "bonding" with others is to share opinions about mutual acquaintances. As a manager, it is very important that you NOT discuss your opinions about certain staff members with other staff members (even if you consider them to be your friends). The principle of not saying anything about anyone that you wouldn't say to his face is also a useful one to teach to teenagers, who can often be extremely critical about others (due to their own insecurities).

The Golden Rule

You may know the golden rule as "Do unto others as you would have others do unto you." If you apply this strategy to gift giving, you will see that it doesn't always work. One year, my husband bought me a router for my birthday. While Sean loves power tools, I don't even know what a router does. As it turned out, the router was a gag, and the real gift was a beautiful table lamp, by which I could read and write. His gift proved a point, however. I had been hesitant to buy him tools for special occasions because a gift of a table saw didn't seem personal enough *to me*. But, if the intent of the gift were really to make *him* happy, it shouldn't really matter whether *I* thought it was appropriate or not, so long as it was something *he* really wanted.

Therefore, I propose rewriting the golden rule to read, "Do unto others as *they* would have others do unto *them*." This means putting yourself in their shoes. That is not always easy, but keeping in mind the insights about others that can be gleaned from the Myers-Briggs personality types and McGraw's "Ten Common Characteristics" should help you to better understand where others are coming from. The next step is to approach people in the manner that is most comfortable to them, *not necessarily to you*. This doesn't mean pretending to be someone you're not, but it may mean moving out of your own comfort zone sometimes, in order to make someone else feel comfortable enough to develop a trusting relationship with you.

For example, I once had a staff member who was an outspoken extrovert and also physically much larger than I am. I am a fairly soft-spoken introvert and at least a decade younger than this staff member, and it was very difficult for her to take direction from me as her supervisor. Only when I stepped out of my comfort zone to relate to her in a manner that was more comfortable to her (by standing up straight, speaking louder and more directly than I was accustomed to, and making direct eye contact with her) were we able to have an effective working relationship.

Addressing people's personal preferences means not always treating everyone the same. Successful managers are able to channel the individual strengths of their subordinates and don't expect everyone to live up to the same standards. This doesn't mean treating people unfairly. It means treating people as individuals. Covey quotes a successful parent as saying of her children, "Treat them all the same by treating them differently" (1989: 192). The same approach could be applied to staff members and colleagues in a library setting.

COMMUNICATION

In a successful library, communication must flow from the patrons, through the frontline staff all the way up to the director, as well as from administration to subordinates. Here are some strategies to help keep the channels of communication open.

Top Down

The way in which managers communicate with subordinates sets the tone for all interactions within the library. Whether the method of communication is verbal or written, formal or informal, managers should strive to always communicate as though they were "going on record" on behalf of their library.

PROACTIVE VS. REACTIVE LANGUAGE

Our behaviors follow from our attitudes, which are reflected in our language. In libraries we are always looking to recruit volunteers to assist with various projects. It is important to present volunteer tasks as an opportunity to make a difference rather than as another burden that someone will have to take on. Language can convey this distinction as evidenced by the following examples:

An appeal for YA volunteers to read to young children can be framed two very different ways. The first describes the work to be done. The second says WHY the work is important and rewarding:

1. "The library needs teen volunteers to read to kids once a week."
2. "Studies have shown that children who are read to regularly at a young age develop language skills earlier and have more success in school than children who are not read to. Help kids get off to a good start by participating in the library's 'Book Buddies' program."

Figure 1–1
Reactive vs. Proactive Language

Reactive Language	Proactive Language
There's nothing I can do.	Let's look at our alternatives.
That's just the way I am.	I can choose a different approach.
He makes me so mad.	I control my own feelings.
They won't allow that.	I can create an effective presentation.
I have to do that.	I will choose an appropriate response.
I can't.	I choose.
I must.	I prefer.
If only.	I will.

Covey, Stephen R. p. 78. *The 7 Habits of Highly Effective People,* © 1989 Stephen R. Covey. Reprinted with permission from Franklin Covey Co., www.franklincovey.com

Clearly, teens (and adults) are more likely to be motivated by the need that drives the request, rather than by the request itself.

Covey uses the model of reactive vs. proactive language (see Figure 1-1). Reactive language implies a lack of control over circumstances, whereas proactive language chooses to focus on available options:

The language you use is critical because of the notion of "self-fulfilling prophecy." Not only do your words reflect your attitudes, but they also often determine your behavior.

"I" MESSAGES

Most of us are familiar with the model of "I" messages, in which statements are made using the following phrases:

Wmhen . . .
I [feel, become, want, and so on] . . .
Because . . .

This model builds on Covey's concept of proactive language by stating concerns in a descriptive way, rather than accusing or placing blame on others. For example, a staff member is more likely to become defensive if you simply point out that she is late than if you were to state, "When you are late I feel concerned because we all rely on your help through the duration of your shift."

According to Julius Eitington, "In the I message, you are engaging in self-disclosure: You are describing how you feel. Communicating a feeling, as opposed to blaming, finger-pointing, or engaging in a put-down,

Far too many leaders believe that what they do and why they do it must be obvious to everyone in the organization. It never is. Far too many believe that when they announce things, everyone understands. No one does, as a rule. Yet very often one can't bring in people before the decision; there just isn't enough time for discussion or participation. Effective leaders have to spend a little time on making themselves understood. They sit down with their people and say: This is what we were faced with. These are the alternatives we saw, the alternatives we considered. They ask: What is your opinion? Otherwise the organization will say: Don't these dummies at the top know anything? What's going on here? Why haven't they considered this or that? But if you can say, Yes, we considered it, but still reached this decision, people will understand and will go along. They may say we wouldn't have decided that way, but at least upstairs, they just didn't shoot from the hip. (Drucker, 1990: 25–26)

defuses possible hostility on the part of the person receiving the feedback. Most listeners will respect and accept a feeling, whereas they are quite likely to bristle at lectures or accusations" (1997: 89).

FORMAL VS. INFORMAL COMMUNICATION

The appropriate mode of communication will be determined by:

1. your own personal preference
2. the preference of the person with whom you are communicating
3. the situation

If you are the kind of person who feels comfortable expressing yourself in writing, you may be more inclined to write memos or send messages via e-mail to communicate with your staff members. However, if you have a very small staff, if memos are perceived by your staff as too formal, or if your staff members aren't comfortable with technology, these methods might not be the best choice. A former colleague expressed her dismay when her new boss started e-mailing her messages . . .while they were sitting next to each other in their shared office! However, if my friend were engrossed in a project from which she didn't want to be interrupted, e-mail might have been the appropriate choice for her boss.

There are no hard-and-fast rules about how to communicate, except to constantly weigh the three factors listed above and to adjust your strategy if it doesn't seem to be working.

Covering All Your Bases

The most common complaint in every library I've ever worked in was a lack of communication. Therefore, I don't think it is possible to communicate *too much*. While managers may need to be selective in the type of information they distribute, to insure that it is important, relevant, and not confidential, it is not overkill to post an agenda to a meeting, discuss the issues during the meeting, hand out minutes after the meeting, and follow up with individuals about particular topics. Even though this sort of redundancy may become tedious to you, staff members will appreciate feeling like they are part of the loop.

Taking Advantage of the Grapevine

Managers often view "the grapevine" as a negative thing, and it certainly can be harmful when used to spread gossip or rumors. However, Nigel Nicholson, professor of organizational behavior at the London Business School suggests that gossip may help to reinforce social relationships. "A person huddled in a corner with a colleague, telling him some piece of minor sensation about a common acquaintance is grooming—letting him know he is important and liked enough to be trusted with a confidence" (Kleiman, 2000: G1).

Toon suggests that managers can take advantage of the grapevine "to provide information to staff in an informal and nonthreatening manner"

Gossip: A Career Management Tool

Not all gossip is bad. In fact, the grapevine can be a valuable source of information to help you in your career. Consider that some gossip can be intentional leaks of information you should know or that the grapevine can help you cultivate sources of information. Here's how to make the grapevine work for you:

- **Listen actively.** There's no need to comment on anything. But if you keep an ear out, you may pick up information that could help you, like expected layoffs or an opening in another department.
- **Don't send out a holier-than-thou attitude.** If people perceive that you consider gossip beneath you, they'll cut you out.
- **Don't add grist for the mill.** It could come back to haunt you.
- **Respond carefully.** Even a harmless note of agreement could be misinterpreted.

Library Mosaics, July/August 2000: 19. Permission to reprint courtesy of Raymond Roney.

(1995: 142). It can also be useful to keep your ears tuned to the rumor mill. Although managers should certainly encourage staff members to communicate with them directly, unfortunately the grapevine is sometimes a useful way for supervisors to learn the true feelings of their staff members in order to be able to address them. For example, if you hear that one of your staff members whose performance hasn't been up to par has been having serious marital problems, that may factor in your decision about how or when to address the issue.

However, if staff members are complaining to you directly about the actions of their colleagues, they should first be encouraged to address those concerns directly to the person in question. If they are unable to resolve the situation on their own, it may be appropriate for you, as the supervisor, to meet with both parties to help negotiate a solution. If the situation affects the entire department, then it should be addressed at a departmental meeting when all staff are present.

Bottom Up

My favorite model for a library hierarchy turns the traditional hierarchy on its head, placing the patrons at the top, dictating their needs to the frontline staff, who make suggestions to the middle managers, who inform upper-level administration, who make changes in policy in order to respond to the patrons' desires. In this model, the patron is the boss, and the manager answers to the staff. This makes sense to me for libraries, since everyone's ultimate goal is to serve the patron.

Adopting an inverted hierarchy structure in a library involves a global rethinking of the traditional management structure. Everyone must understand that the customer is in charge. Frontline staff need to be empowered to make decisions that best support the customers' needs. These decisions should be communicated to managers so changes in policy can be made to accommodate patron desires. And administrators need to understand and respect that, on many levels, the public-service staff may be more in touch with the patrons' perspective on library services than those behind the scenes.

INFORMATION-BASED ORGANIZATIONS

Peter Drucker alludes to the inverted hierarchy concept in describing his approach to managing nonprofit organizations. He maintains that:

> The non-profit must be information-based. It must be structured around information that flows up from the individuals doing the work to the people at the top—the ones who are, in the end, accountable—and around information flowing down, too. (1990: 182)

> The most important thing to *do* is to build the organization around information and communication instead of around hierarchy. Everybody in the non-profit institution—all the way up and down—should be expected to take information responsibility. Everyone needs to learn to ask two questions: What information do I need to do *my* job—from whom, when, how? And: What information do I owe others so that they can do *their* job, in what form, and when? (Drucker, 1990: 115)

This model of an information-based organization is particularly appropriate for libraries because information is what we are all about. And effective communication is the only way we are able to convey that information.

COACHING

Anyone who has ever visited Seattle has probably seen the "fish throwers" of Pike Place Market Fish Company. They entertain crowds by singing, performing skits, interacting with customers, and throwing fish to each other to fill orders. The employees of the market are given the option to coach and be coached at work. If they agree to do this, they are held accountable by their colleagues to always act in accordance with their organization's mission. They also agree to hold others accountable to do the same. They do this through coaching each other by providing regular feedback (Lundin et al., 2000).

This model of coaching can work equally well with a Teen Advisory Board as with staff. The key element, however, is permission. People need to decide, of their own accord, that they want to receive feedback from each other in order for the system to function smoothly. The standards that people are held accountable to should also be clearly defined and preferably created by the group. These can take the form of "group norms" or standards of behavior that everyone agrees to respect. They should also take into account the library, department, or organization's mission, service priorities, and policies and procedures.

Supervisors are coaches by default and are expected to give feedback whether or not it is invited. According to William Pfeiffer, the goals of coaching are to solve problems and improve performance:

1. **Problem-solving** processes are *counseling, mentoring,* and *tutoring* interactions. Problem-solving processes begin when either the

> **Useful Resource Tip:**
> An excellent source for additional information about coaching is
> *Masterful Coaching: Extraordinary Results by Impacting People and the
> Way They Think and Work Together* by Robert Hargrove.

employee or the manager perceives an employee's need. Such processes can be initiated either by the employee or by the manager.

2. **Performance-improvement** processes are *confronting* or *challenging* interactions. They take place in order to alter employee behavior—to correct a performance deficiency or to present a new
task or challenge. Confronting or challenging processes are always
initiated by the manager. (1994: 139)

Observation

Once, when I was in college, I was so distraught over the fact that my
boyfriend and I were about to break up that I was sitting in his dorm
room with him and his friends for a full 15 minutes before I realized
they had piled up all his clothes and furniture on top of his bed! This is
an extreme example of our ability to overlook important visual cues from
others.

Most of the time, the signals that people give off are not as obvious
as piling all their furniture on their bed, but careful observation can determine a lot about people—perhaps even more than they know about
themselves. Robert Hargrove suggests that the role of a coach is to ob-
serve people's strategies for approaching situations and to intervene when
those strategies break down. He states that "people cannot see the dis-
crepancy between what they think they are doing and what they are actually doing. In the same sense, people often do not have the capacity
to see themselves as others see them or detect their own errors and eliminate them" (1995: 148).

When I was assistant director of the Missoula Public Library, I tried
to always be patient and polite in my speech towards staff members regardless of how I felt about whatever they might be saying. Although I
was successful in doing so, a colleague pointed out that I would sometimes roll my eyes when I became frustrated with someone in a meeting. I was horrified to learn I was doing this, but grateful the error was
pointed out to me so I could become more aware I was doing it and
take pains to stop it immediately.

Feedback

Once a coach has carefully observed people's approaches to situations
and identified where their strategies break down, she must provide

constructive feedback in order to meet the goals of problem solving and performance improvement stated above. Hargrove states that an effective coach can help people to "see mistakes as an opportunity rather than as a threat" (1995: 147).

Feedback can take the form of counseling, mentoring, tutoring, and confronting or challenging (Pfeiffer, 1994: 137). To be most effective, feedback should be given on an ongoing basis and not saved up for a performance evaluation. It should be done one-on-one (and not in a group) and should address specific issues in a timely manner.

Both positive and negative feedback are essential to healthy work relationships. Feedback on work performance should always focus on concrete issues and events, not on individual personalities. However, the communication strategies and suggestions for understanding other perspectives discussed earlier in this chapter can be effective tools in providing constructive feedback to staff and teens alike.

TROUBLESHOOTING

Strategies for troubleshooting specific situations will be given within the chapters that deal with the specific situations. A few general strategies, however, can apply to all relationships.

Problem Solving and Conflict Resolution

Most management experts recommend finding common ground and separating the issues from the people in working to solve problems and resolve conflicts. Stephen Covey advocates for finding a win-win solution to problems using the following four-step process:

First, see the problem from the other point of view. Really seek to understand and to give expression to the needs and concerns of the other party as well as or better than they can themselves.

Second, identify the key issues and concerns (not positions) involved.

Third, determine what results would constitute a fully acceptable solution.

And fourth, identify possible new options to achieve those results.

Covey, Stephen R. p. 233. *The 7 Habits of Highly Effective People,* © 1989 Stephen R. Covey. Reprinted with permission from Franklin Covey Co., www.franklincovey.com

This is an approach that librarians frequently use in response to patrons who advocate censorship. First, we listen to the patron's concerns, then commend them on taking an interest in what their children are accessing at the library. Thirdly, we ask what they would like to see happen as a result of their concern, and finally, we offer them other options, such as completing a request for consideration form, or, in some cases, restricting Internet access on their child's card.

Roger Fisher and William Ury warn against "bargaining over positions" in their book *Getting to Yes: Negotiation Agreement Without Giving In*. They propose a four-step process to conflict resolution that focuses on people, interests, options, and criteria:

- Separate the people from the problem.
- Focus on interests, not positions.
- Generate a variety of possibilities before deciding what to do.
- Insist the result be based on some objective standard. (1983: 11)

Insisting that results be based on some objective standard is another way of defining the ultimate goal that you all hope to achieve (in such a way that it will be recognizable to all, once you get there). For example, in a public library, reference staff may view teen use of the reading room as disruptive to adult patrons, while Young Adult staff want teens to feel welcome anywhere in the library. Through separating the people from the problem and focusing on interests not positions, it may be determined that the real issue is what type of behavior is appropriate for the reading room.

Possibilities for resolving the problem might include creating a Young Adult space in a noisier area of the library where teen socializing won't be disruptive to adult patrons; posting "quiet area" signs in the reading room and enforcing that policy equitably; reconsidering whether it is truly feasible for the reading room to be a quiet space in this particular library, and so on. And finally, the objective standard to measure whether the solution decided upon is effective may be a survey of adult and young adult patrons to make sure that the library is able to meet the needs of each group.

In order to use the above methods effectively, the manager must function as a neutral facilitator, helping to build consensus rather than favoring one side over another. This means having more invested in a peaceful and effective solution to problems than in any particular outcome.

Dealing with Difficult People

Rick Brinkman and Rick Kirschner point out that you have four choices when interacting with difficult people:

1. You can stay and do nothing.
2. You can vote with your feet.
3. You can change your attitude about your difficult person.
4. You can change your behavior. (1994: 12)

Two essential skills that they recommend are blending and redirecting. "*Blending* is any behavior by which you reduce the differences between you and another in order to meet them where they are and move to more common ground. The result of blending is an increase in rapport. *Redirecting* is any behavior by which you use that rapport to change the trajectory of that interaction" (1994: 38) The theory behind these

---

When You Communicate with Problem People

Your Goal: Speak to Be Understood

Action Plan

1. Monitor your tone of voice.
2. State your positive intent.
3. Tactfully interrupt interruptions.
4. Tell your truth.
5. Be ready to listen. (Brinkman and Kirschner, 1994: 61)

When Your Problem Person Is Talking

Your Goal: Listen to Understand

Action Plan

1. Blend visibly and audibly.
2. Backtrack some of their own words.
3. Clarify their meaning, intent, and criteria.
4. Summarize what you've heard.
5. Confirm to find out if you got it right. (Brinkman and Kirschner, 1994: 47)

Brinkman, Rick and Rick Kirschner. *Dealing With People You Can't Stand: How to Bring Out the Best in People at Their Worst.* © 1994 Rick Brinkman and Rick Kirschner. New York: McGraw-Hill, Inc. Reproduced with permission of the McGraw-Hill Companies.

Dissent [. . .] is essential for effective decision making. Feuding and bickering are not. In fact, they must not be tolerated. They destroy the spirit of an organization. (Drucker, 1990: 114)

strategies is that it is easier to get along with people if they view you to be like them. By blending with your body language, words, and tone of voice, you put the difficult person at ease, which allows you to more easily redirect the interaction.

When dealing with difficult people it is helpful to focus not on the person, but on the behavior. Everyone can be "difficult" in certain situations. "Difficult people" just tend to exhibit inappropriate behavior more frequently than others.

Often inappropriate behavior stems from fear or insecurity. It is important for a manager to try and understand people's motivations for behaving the way that they do and to realize that their behavior may be a reflection of their own insecurity about meeting the expectations they have set for themselves.

Resistant behavior can also reveal the underlying values of staff members in a particular situation. For example, a resistance to learning how to use a new piece of equipment may indicate not so much a discomfort with technology as a fear of change and a concern that they won't be able to master the skills necessary to accommodate that change. An employee who doesn't want to learn how to create Web pages might be teamed up with another employee who enjoys doing this. If they work together to create a site on a topic that interests the resistant employee, this might provide an opportunity to master the necessary skills in a fun way.

Using the communication strategies introduced earlier in this chapter can help managers to listen effectively enough to detect the "real issues" behind inappropriate behavior and address those issues directly in their approach to the situation.

While individual instances of inappropriate behavior can be annoying (and sometimes be cause for disciplinary action), more pervasive griping can indicate deeper problems within the organization. Drucker states that "most people think that feuding and bickering bespeak 'personality conflicts.' They rarely do. They usually are symptoms of the need to change the organization. It may have grown very fast and in the process outgrown its structure; nobody quite knows what he or she is responsible for. Then people begin to blame each other . . ." (1990: 114). Steps should be taken immediately to resolve pervasive conflict among staff

Figure 1–2
Characteristics of Admired Leaders

Characteristic	1993 U.S. Respondents Percentage of People Selecting	1987 U.S. Respondents Percentage of People Selecting
Honest	87	83
Forward-looking	71	62
Inspiring	68	58
Competent	58	67
Fair-minded	49	40
Supportive	46	32
Broad-minded	41	37
Intelligent	38	43
Straightforward	34	34
Courageous	33	27
Dependable	32	32
Cooperative	30	25
Imaginative	28	34
Caring	27	26
Mature	14	23
Determined	13	20
Ambitious	10	21
Loyal	10	11
Self-controlled	5	13
Independent	5	10

Kouzes, James M. and Barry Z. Posner. Copyright © 1993. *Credibility: How Leaders Gain and Lose It, Why People Demand It.* San Francisco: Jossey-Bass Inc.: 14. Reprinted by permission of John Wiley & Sons, Inc.

members. Clarifying the organization's mission and people's roles within it may be an effective way to address the underlying issues.

LEADERSHIP AND SUPERVISION

Managers are expected to serve as mentors, who model the types of behavior they expect from their subordinates, as well as teachers, who guide and instruct their staff members to live up to their potential. What follows are a few strategies to develop these relationships.

Socializing with Subordinates

The old adage "it's lonely at the top" can be true unless managers are able to develop appropriate social relationships with their subordinates. As has been implied throughout this chapter, the most effective managers are those who take a personal interest in their staff and colleagues, which may include socializing at work as well as outside of the workplace.

Kathy Toon emphasizes the benefit of eating lunch together, whether it be under informal circumstances or in planned "theme lunches." "Meals are often used by business people to court a client or make a deal. Eating together puts everyone on the same level and may serve as an icebreaker for discussions. One of the practices that has been very successful in cementing good communication and rapport between departments in some libraries is lunches" (1995: 144).

Social events at work such as birthday parties, baby showers, and so on foster a sense of camaraderie so long as they are provided on an equitable basis. Setting up a care and concerns committee (or alternating party planning among groups of staff members) can help to insure that all special occasions are acknowledged and celebrated. Sending birthday cards to staff members or taking them out to lunch on their birthday are other ways supervisors can show they care (and learn more about their staff members while they're at it). Group outings such as attending a baseball game together or having a cookout can also help staff members feel like they're part of a team.

Although supervisor-subordinate friendships can be tricky, they are often inevitable, particularly in small departments, and can actually be beneficial to the work environment when approached in the right way. Supervisors who are friendly with all their staff members outside of work are less likely to be accused of favoritism than those who develop close friendships with only one or two of their subordinates. All supervisor-subordinate friends should avoid discussing work issues outside of the workplace and under no circumstances should supervisors discuss confidential personnel issues with their subordinates. The issue of confidentiality should be discussed openly between the friends, and both supervisor and subordinate should respect the constraints of their positions within the organization. Supervisors and subordinates should also do their best to avoid allowing their personal information about each other to interfere with their work relationship.

Romantic relationships between supervisors and subordinates should be avoided at all cost. Should such a relationship develop in your department, the most ethical way to approach it is to discuss the situation frankly with the next-level supervisor and arrange for the person who is in the relationship with the supervisor to be supervised by someone else (at least for the duration of the relationship, possibly indefinitely).

The supervisor-subordinate relationship applies to librarians who work with teen groups as well. Although it is useful to be on friendly terms with teens, it is important to keep in mind your role as mentor and library employee when dealing with teens on library time. Although Teen Advisory Board activities often have a social component, because of the intrinsic imbalance of power between teens and librarians it is probably best to avoid developing close individual friendships with teens outside of the library until after they graduate from your library program.

Teen crushes on adult mentors are fairly common and should be handled with as much grace and tact as is possible, while taking pains to make your role clear to everyone involved. It is NEVER appropriate for a librarian to become romantically involved with a teenager whom they have worked with in the library even if that teen has reached the legal age of majority.

Stewardship

The most important role of a supervisor is to make your employees' jobs easier. In order to do this, you must have a thorough understanding of what their job entails (although you do not necessarily have to know how to do it). Covey warns against "gopher delegation," which essentially micromanages the tasks of subordinates. Instead, he proposed a model of "stewardship delegation," which involves "clear, up-front mutual understanding and commitment regarding expectations in five areas"—desired results, guidelines, resources, accountability, and consequences (1989: 174).

Under this model, the employee is responsible for coordinating her own projects, according to the terms mutually agreed upon with her supervisor. The role of the supervisor is to provide resources and support as needed. Drucker recommends asking every one of your subordinates and colleagues, "What am I doing that helps you with your work? What am I doing that hampers you?" and acting on what they tell you (1990: 184). This can be done informally during individual staff meetings or by more formally soliciting feedback in the form of a survey or "supervisor feedback" form. Either way, be sure to take staff comments seriously and work to bring about change in the areas they suggest.

REFERENCES

Brinkman, Rick, and Rick Kirschner. 1994. *Dealing with People You Can't Stand: How to Bring Out the Best in People at Their Worst.* New York: McGraw-Hill.

Covey, Stephen R. 1989. *The 7 Habits of Highly Effective People: Restoring the Character Ethic*. New York: Simon & Schuster.

Drucker, Peter F. 1990. *Managing the Non-profit Organization*. New York: HarperCollins.

Eitington, Julius E. 1997. *The Winning Manager: Leadership Skills for Greater Innovation, Quality, and Employee Commitment*. Houston: Gulf Publishing Company.

Fisher, Roger and William Ury. Edited by Bruce Patton. 1983. *Getting to YES: Negotiation Agreement Without Giving In*. Boston: Houghton Mifflin. New York: Penguin Books.

"Gossip: A Career Management Tool." 2000. *Library Mosaics* 11, no. 4 (July/August): 19.

Hargrove, Robert. 1995. *Masterful Coaching: Extraordinary Results by Impacting People and the Way They Think and Work Together*. San Diego: Pfeiffer & Co.

Kleiman, Carol. 2000. "Gossiping Is Only Natural." *Missoulian*, 15 October, Section G (reprinted from the *Chicago Tribune*).

Kouzes, James M., and Barry Z. Posner. 1993. *Credibility: How Leaders Gain and Lose It, Why People Demand It*. San Francisco: Jossey-Bass.

Lundin, Stephen C., Harry Paul, and John Christensen. 2000. *Fish! A Remarkable Way to Boost Morale and Improve Results*. New York: Hyperion.

McGraw, Phillip C. 1999. *Life Strategies: Doing What Works, Doing What Matters*. New York: Hyperion.

Myers, Isabel Briggs, and Mary H. McCaulley. 1985. *A Guide to the Development and Use of the Myers-Briggs Type Indicator*. Palo Alto, Calif.: Consulting Psychologists Press.

Pfeiffer, J. William, ed. 1994. "The Coaching Process." In *Theories and Models in Applied Behavioral Science: Group, 26*. San Diego: Pfeiffer & Company.

Robbins, Carla Anne. 2001. "Rules-Happy Cabinet: Rumsfeld, Powell and O'Neill Weigh In." *Wall Street Journal*, 2 March.

Tieger, Paul D., and Barbara Barron-Tieger. 1992. *Do What You Are: Discover the Perfect Career for You Through the Secrets of Personality Type*. New York: Little, Brown.

Toon, Kathy. 1995. "Establishing Staff Relations." In *Youth Services Librarians as Managers: A How-To Guide from Budgeting to Personnel*. Edited by Kathleen Staerkel, Mary Fellows, and Sue McCleaf Nespeca. Chicago: American Library Association.

Chapter 2

Managing Young Adults

THE CUSTOMER IS ALWAYS RIGHT?
YOUNG ADULT PATRONS

Perhaps the most basic and widely accepted tenet of customer service is the contention that "the customer is always right." But does this really apply to teenage "customers" as well? The retail world gives us contradictory messages—many companies actively target the young adult population (and their increasing amounts of discretionary spending money), while other establishments hang signs prohibiting more than two teenagers from entering the store at the same time.

In libraries, we're often not sure how to approach young adults. One of the tools that many Young Adult services trainers use is an activity in which librarians are asked what do they do with a child when they are getting ready to cross the street, and to stand and indicate, with their hand, how tall a child is. None of the participants ever have any trouble with this activity. When they are asked to do the same with young adults, however, the participants usually break into nervous laughter when they realize that they don't really know how tall a YA is (they vary so much in stages of development!) or what to do with them when you cross the street (or perhaps at any other time).

Teens are in an awkward place between childhood and adulthood, and this makes it somewhat difficult to know how to interact with them. As Lillian Shapiro states in her article, "Equals or Enemies?: Librarians and Young Adults,"

Among the problems in young adult library service today is that those adults who work with youth, especially in schools, are the products of a society which has set up rigid divisions between child, youth, and adult. Unquestioning and undeviating respect for authority, a highly valued principle, is antithetical to education which supposedly encourages a pursuit of the truth, a mind free to explore among all kinds of information in order to find one's own answer. (1997: 113–114)

Perhaps the key to successful Young Adult services may be in allowing those divisions to be less rigid and in developing a more collaborative means of interaction. When in doubt about how to approach a young adult in the library, it is always safest to err up and treat him as you would an adult (rather than as a child). Show respect for your young adult patrons by treating them the way you would expect to be treated. Joel Shoemaker and Patrick Jones, authors of *Do It Right! Best Practices for Serving Young Adults in School and Public Libraries* (Neal-Schuman: Teens @ the Library Series, 2001), refer to this as the "fast food" model of customer service, "smile, greet, thank, repeat."

US VS. THEM: THE GENERATION GAP

Although it is often helpful to recall your own experience as an adolescent, in order to better empathize with your YA customers, it is also important to understand the difference between your generation and theirs.

How We Are the Same

Adolescents today go through the exact same physical and emotional changes we all went through when we were that age. Their basic psychological needs (acceptance, independence, identity, sexuality, and so on) haven't changed. If you take a moment to think back on your own adolescence, you may find that many of the themes are identical to those your children or your young adult patrons are dealing with today.

In many respects, the developmental tasks of young adults today are quite similar to those of past generations. Mid-adolescents still need a healthy family and social environment to maintain them while they carve out their own identity. They need a testing ground of active, caring peers and adults to help them answer the questions, "Who am I?" and "What will I do?" Mid-to-late adolescents need to have a sense of fidelity. They need to reconcile their sexual and aggressive impulses with a well-developed conscience. And they need to feel they have done the work necessary to move into a meaningful adulthood. (Holmes, 1995: 63)

We can all relate to young adults because we have all been there (although many of us have tried to forget that part of our lives). Remembering our own experiences as teenagers can help us to better understand the sometimes apparently contradictory behaviors of the young adults we see in the library.

How We Are Different

Young Adult librarians, regardless of their age, know that today's world is different from the world we grew up in. Holmes outlines major changes that have occurred in the following areas since the 1950s (I have added some of my observations to this list as well):

> **family life**—The number of single-parent families has drastically increased, as has the number of parents in the workforce.
> **schools**—Schools have gotten larger, students commute farther to school, and school violence is receiving more media attention.
> **sexuality**—Today's teenagers become sexually active earlier and have sex with many more partners. There is also evidence that puberty is occurring at an earlier age for both males and females. The AIDS epidemic has increased awareness (and risks) of sexually transmitted diseases and the precautions necessary to avoid them.
> **drugs**—Illegal drug use has increased, and the use or abuse of alcohol continues to be a problem for many teens.
> **technology**—Television and computers have exposed today's teens to new ideas, situations, and products. New formats such as MP3s make music more portable, and some lyrics have become more explicit and sometimes threatening. (Holmes, 1995: 149–151)

As youth services workers, we have undoubtedly observed some of these generational differences firsthand and may be able to add a few more trends to the list. Perhaps the primary difference is that teenagers in previous generations were sheltered to some extent from the adult world. With the increased incidence of divorce and single-parent families, today's teens are more likely to be required to function as adults, and they share many of the same pressures and concerns of society at large.

UNDERSTANDING YOUNG ADULTS

Although teens and adults may be dealing with similar issues, young adults have the added challenge of addressing them while simultaneously enduring all of the physical and emotional changes that are characteris-

Figure 2–1
Individuation: The Teen Life Task

Many life tasks are inherent in child growth and development. These tasks may be physical, intellectual, emotional, social, psychological, or spiritual. During adolescence, individuation is the primary task, as outlined below:

1. Adolescents have a need to find out who they are, how they are different from their family, how they feel about things, what their own values are, and what they think about things. This process of separation from the family in preparation for an independent adulthood is called individuation.
2. Individuation usually looks like rebellion to parents. Although most parents worry when their teenagers rebel, it would be more appropriate to worry if they didn't. Teenagers must begin their separation from their family, and rebellion gives them the energy to do this. At first, teens may rebel by looking at what is important to us or what we want, then doing exactly the opposite. Later, they may rebel in other ways—but at first, individuation is primarily a reaction against their parents.
3. Whether they like it or not, adolescents are maturing physically and sexually, undergoing biological processes that are essentially out of their control. In addition to the tumultuous, contradictory feelings these major changes cause, adolescents may feel anxiety regarding their rate of change—they may feel their physical maturation is too quick or too slow in relation to that of their peers. (Most parents would prefer their kids to mature slowly, but nature has her own patterns!)
4. The physical maturation process, with its sudden and powerful hormonal changes, causes mood swings. Without premeditation, teens are delightful one minute and biting our heads off the next. In addition, some teens are in such a rapid rate of physical growth that they experience real "growing pains" where their bodies actually hurt.
5. Teens need to work out their relationships with peers to find out if and how they fit in. Friendships take the place of time spent with the family. While this helps teens in their task of separation, it is often interpreted by parents as rejection or rebellion.
6. Teens have a strong desire to find out what they're capable of— the need to test their power and importance in the world. This means that they want to decide what they can do for themselves

Figure 2–1
Continued

without being directed and ordered. However, some teens find this so intimidating that they *want* others, usually their peers, to tell them what to do.

7. Teens have a great need for privacy so they can work out a lot of the already-mentioned tasks without an audience. Since their rate of development moves so fast and is out of their own control, it can be embarrassing to have their parents watching and knowing. In addition, to figure out what's important to them, teens may do things their parents wouldn't approve of before deciding for themselves that they might not want to do them either. They need the room to test these things without getting in trouble or disappointing their parents.

8. During this period, teens tend to put their parents down and try to show them how "stupid" they are. Sometimes teens act embarrassed around their parents and families in public or may even refuse to be seen with them. The affection that may have been a normal part of family life may suddenly become taboo.

9. Teens think of themselves as omnipotent and all-knowing. Parents who try to tell them how to dress or eat or what they can or can't do just don't seem to understand that the teen *never* gets sick, *doesn't* get cold, *doesn't* need sleep and can live *forever* on junk food or not eat *at all.*

tic of this time of life. In order to effectively manage young adults, it is important to understand the physiological and psychological factors that influence their behavior.

Adolescent Development

Many excellent books have been written on adolescent development. One in particular that I would recommend for librarians is *Helping Teenagers Into Adulthood* by George Holmes. Holmes divides adolescence into three categories (early, middle, and late) and describes the social, physical, and behavioral changes that occur in each stage. He also offers specific strategies for dealing with YAs at each of these developmental stages.

The Five Developmental Tasks of Adolescence
1. separating from old ties
2. creating new attachments
3. establishing a mature sexual identity
4. formulating new ideas and ideals
5. consolidating character (Siegler, 1997: 16–17)

The wide variations in maturity in the group that librarians refer to as young adults (Young Adult Library Services Association's [YALSA] defined age range is 12 to 18) is not often acknowledged or addressed in the professional literature. However, the needs and interests of a sixth grader are vastly different from those of a senior in high school. Although there are benefits to grouping junior high or middle school students with high school students (particularly in the public library, where staff to serve each individual group are usually nonexistent), there may also be times when it is more appropriate to host programs that target a particular subset of "young adults" only. Some libraries even separate their YA collections into "middle school" and "high school" sections or target older teens in the YA area and serve the needs of younger teens in the children's department.

Teen Stressors

Parents of teenagers know only too well how incredibly *busy* they are. The parents of one of my former Teen Library Council members used to require their daughter to schedule relaxation time every day, because if they didn't she would literally have been running from one activity to the next from the time she woke up in the morning until the time that she went to bed (probably too late) at night. Teens who are concerned about getting into college may overextend themselves in an attempt to prove themselves worthy to the college of their choice. Unfortunately, the young adult's emotional well-being may suffer as a result. In addition to the internal changes that take place during adolescence, most teens experience some degree of stress from external factors:

> **time commitments**—Like adults, many teens today are overcommitted. They juggle school and homework with sports, extracurricular activities, jobs, and social events. Trying to do "everything" in a limited amount of time can be a huge source of stress for young adults.
> **peer pressure**—Most teens are concerned about trying to look

or act "right" in order to be accepted by their peers. Even those teens who "refuse to conform" are responding to societal pressures to act like their peers.

school stressors—Contrary to popular belief, even teens who don't do well in school often experience stress about their grades. Many students are also very concerned about getting accepted to the college of their choice. Competition, intimidation, and fear of violence are also very real concerns in schools today.

family pressures—Problems with parents and siblings can be a source of stress for YAs, as can the desire to live up to parental expectations.

money—In an increasingly consumerist society, the need to earn money to buy the "right" things can also cause stress for teens.

> Experimenting with various life styles, with drug cultures, religious sects, with militant stances, and radical politics, our young adults are, at one and the same time, the subject of sermons despairing of their irresponsibility and self-destructiveness, and the object of envy on the part of their elders (who should be wiser) because of their freedom of dress, sexual codes and refusal to make permanent commitments to self or family. (Shapiro, 1997: 113)

The admiration (and sometimes envy) of teens is something that is not often discussed in professional library literature. But I believe that our society tends to judge teens so harshly because we secretly desire to be more like them in some ways. Young adults are often more passionate in their convictions than adults and more willing to stand up for their beliefs. They are also freer than their elders to experiment with who they are and how they want to be perceived. Since so many adult experiences are new to them, they may be more willing to try new things and less fearful of making mistakes. However, as the preceding list of adolescent stressors indicates, the "best years of their lives" may not really be as carefree as they seem to us from the outside.

Risk-Taking Behavior

> Adolescents take risks as a way of developing and defining themselves. They do this by taking on new challenges in areas that they often understand very little about, engaging in behaviors with results that range from devastating to extremely positive. *Risk-taking is the major tool that adolescents use to shape their identities.* (Ponton, 1997: 273)

According to Lynn Ponton, author of *The Romance of Risk: Why Teenagers Do the Things They Do*, "Just as infants are bound to mature and one day start walking, adolescents are going to engage in risk-taking, an important, inevitable process through which they come to understand themselves and life" (1997: 274). Risk-taking behavior can range from structured and supervised physical challenges to eating disorders, sexual promiscuity, and drug abuse. Of course, children take risks as well. However, the risks that teens take are often greater as a result of the bigger tools they have at their disposal, such as faster transportation, alcohol and drugs, and greater access to the wider world.

Traditional cultures offered "coming of age" rituals to their adolescents, in which teens were expected to overcome obstacles in order to "prove" their adulthood. While confirmations, bar and bat mitzvahs, and graduation ceremonies may attempt to serve the same role in mainstream society, adolescents still seek out ways to "prove themselves" to their peers, parents, and others.

Sports, grades, sex, getting a driver's license, getting into college or getting a job, and leaving home are some of the ways that today's teens try to forge an adult identity. It is important for adults to acknowledge the "rite of passage" of adolescence—to encourage positive challenges and be aware of the warning signs of destructive risk-taking behaviors

WARNING SIGNS

While some behavior that generally isn't welcome in a library is actually quite normal for adolescents (such as talking loudly, travelling in groups, slouching, and putting feet on furniture), certain behaviors can indicate that a teenager has a more serious problem. Although not all states require librarians to report suspected abuse or neglect, I feel that we have a moral obligation to do so. And while it is not a librarian's job to diagnose illness of any kind, if you have good reason to believe that a young adult is depressed or suicidal, abusing substances, or suffering from an eating disorder or other serious problem, it may be appropriate to refer her to an agency that can provide the type of support she needs.

Young Adult Trends

It can be helpful to think about young adults as a separate cultural group—with their own language, dress code, and standards of behavior. Like any other outsider working with a minority group, Young Adult librarians and school media specialists need to learn about the unique characteristics of the population they serve.

Some characteristics (such as physical changes and the emotional re-

> **The Warning Signs of Possible Dysfunction**
> The following list is not inclusive but should serve as a guide to determine if behavior is more abnormal than normal. Any of these behaviors might warrant professional help when they represent a pattern rather than isolated incidents.
> 1. When, for extended periods of time, kids tell us in words that they are unhappy, depressed, feel like killing themselves, hate us, have no friends, and so on. Most teens will express these feelings in isolated incidents that will last only a few hours or a few days.
> 2. When kids exhibit some of the signs of depression, like loss of appetite, sleeping more than usual, not taking care of their person, spending a lot of time alone or in their rooms, abuse of chemicals, and general despair.
> 3. When kids start "acting out" extreme behaviors such as stealing, setting fires, becoming physically violent, completely giving up in school, throwing up, abusing chemicals, or leaving drug paraphernalia around the house.
> 4. When kids exhibit signs of suicide attempts, cut or mutilate their bodies, get pregnant, or stay "loaded" all the time.
> 5. When kids start getting their life in order and giving away their possessions to prepare for suicide.
>
> *Helping Teenagers Into Adulthood*, Holmes, George. Copyright © 1995 by George Holmes. Reproduced with permission of Greenwood Publishing Group, Inc., Westport, CT.

actions that accompany them) of young adults remain fairly consistent from generation to generation, but each generation of YAs is also marked by its own unique fads and trends. These range from fashion and music interests to political and societal concerns to fundamental information needs.

> In *The 7 Habits of Highly Effective People*, Steven Covey talks about a friend of his who has a son who loves baseball. The man spent over six months taking his son to see every major league team play one game. When he returned, someone asked him if he liked baseball that much. "No," he replied, "but I like my son that much." (1989: 191)

Young Adult librarians need to keep up with these trends by talking to teenagers, reading their magazines, watching their TV shows, and listening to their music. I am not implying that librarians should try to act like young adults, but in order to fully understand the population they serve, they need to take at least some interest in those things that interest teens.

Young Adult department supervisors (or Young Adult "Lone Rangers"—as Jane Byczek and I referred to those librarians who are the only ones responsible for serving young adults in their libraries in an article we wrote for *VOYA* in June 1998) should also make the most of demographic and survey information to learn as much as they can about young adult trends and the characteristics of the teens in their area. Information about (local and national) teen needs and interests should drive library resources and programs directed towards this age group.

THE INFLUENCE OF TECHNOLOGY ON THE NET GENERATION

One of the things that sets *this* generation of YAs apart from previous generations is their immersion in technology from the time they were born. Many young adults today are more comfortable with technology than the adults who are expected to teach and lead them. Don Tapscott refers to the children of the baby boomers (born between 1977 and 1997) as the "Net Generation." In his fascinating book *Growing Up Digital*, Tapscott describes how technology has shaped today's teens and how their facility with technology will shape the world of the future.

> The baby boom was the biggest population wave ever—until it was eclipsed by the Net Generation. The N-Generation now represents 30 percent of the population, compared to the boomers' 29 percent [....] But what makes N-Geners unique is not just their large numbers, but that they are growing up during the dawn of a completely new interactive medium of communication. Just as the much more limited medium of television influenced the values and culture of the baby boomers, a new force is helping to shape the N-Gen wave. They are spending their formative years in a context and environment fundamentally different from their parents. (Tapscott, 1998: 15)

It is paramount that Young Adult librarians and media specialists learn all they can about the technological world that teens inhabit. Whether or not we share their enthusiasm about the Internet, PDAs, chat rooms, and agents, we need to understand these technologies well enough to

Figure 2–2
Relationship Between N-Gen Culture and
the New Culture of Work

N-gen Culture	The New Culture Of Work
Fierce independence	Molecularization
Emotional, intellectual openness	Openness
A culture of inclusion	Collaboration, collective leadership
Free expression and strong views	Internetworking for organizational consciousness
A culture of innovation	Innovation in everything
Preoccupation with maturity	People judged on contribution
A culture of investigation	New authorities
Immediacy	The real-time firm
Sensitivity to corporate interest	N-Gen capital
A culture of authentication	Trustworthiness and trust

Tapscott, Don. 1998. *Growing Up Digital: The Rise of the Net Generation.* New York: McGraw-Hill: 211. Reproduced with permission of the McGraw-Hill Companies.

be able to talk about their appeal and take advantage of their capabilities to help us provide more effective library services.

There are many books and classes available on all aspects of technology, but the easiest way to learn about those services and gadgets that appeal most to the YAs you serve is to ask them to show you.

We [. . .] have an unparalleled opportunity to learn from [the Net Generation] for personal and business success and for social development. The people, companies, and nations which succeed in the new economy will be those who listen to their children. We can listen to their views on the world. We can learn from their effortless mastery and application of new tools. By listening and responding to their frustrations of being denied adequate tools and support, we can envision and enact the new partnerships required for a new age. (Tapscott, 1998: 13)

INTERACTING WITH YOUNG ADULTS

The most important thing to remember about interacting with young adults is to treat them as people. Children expect you to treat them as

> **Talking to Teenagers**
> Learn to listen.
> Be ready to respond.
> Ask for their advice or opinion.
> Keep an open mind.
> Don't feel you must always try to protect them.
> Talk about feelings as well as facts.
> (Fenwick and Smith, 1996: 57–58)

children—to guide them in decision making and to tell them what to do. As teenagers begin to develop a unique sense of self, they are no longer content to be treated as children. Although they are not yet adults, they deserve to be treated as unique individuals, capable of making their own decisions. Remember, when in doubt, err up.

Making Connections

In *Adolescence: The Survival Guide for Parents and Teenagers*, Elizabeth Fenwick and Dr. Tony Smith recommend using the four C's to connect with teens: compassion, communication, comprehension, and competence (Fenwick and Smith, 1996: 78–83). This is good advice for librarians as well. Since teens are often self-absorbed and shy around adults they don't know, the onus is on the librarian to establish connections with teens. Take the time to talk to kids who come into the YA area. Ask questions beyond the standard "Is there anything I can help you find?" to get to know their interests. But don't be too intrusive—respect their privacy if they don't seem eager to talk to you. Over time, most teens will open up and grow to trust adults who regularly express genuine interest in their well-being.

Youth Participation Groups

Perhaps the easiest way to connect with young adults is to involve them in an advisory group. Known as Teen Advisory Boards (TAB), Youth Advisory Councils (YAC), and so on, these groups involve teens in planning Young Adult (and sometimes other) library services.

Establishing a youth participation group is the best Young Adult management tool I know of. It allows the librarian to get to know local teens and to become familiar with their needs and interests. It encourages teens to get involved with the library and to meet new people. It provides library staff with a better understanding of real young adults and allows teens to have a sense of responsibility and accomplishment.

YA-YAAC

Purpose: To allow teen library advisory groups and the librarians who coordinate them in school and public libraries to share information and ideas. All those groups with e-mail addresses or fax numbers that are included in the National Youth Participation Database are subscribers of YA-YAAC. The Youth Participation Committee is also included.

Uses: Networking
Exchanging ideas
Discussing common problems and seeking solutions
Encouraging youth participation in library activities

To subscribe: Send a message to listproc@ala.org. Leave the subject line blank. For the message, type "Subscribe YA-YAAC first name last name."

To unsubscribe: Send a message to listproc@ala1.ala.org. For the message, type "Unsubscribe YA-YAAC."

From: 4 July 2001. "YALSA Mailing Lists and Web Sites." Young Adult Library Services Association. www.ala.org/yalsa/professional/yalsalists.html

---

There are numerous books and articles that address the logistics of setting up a youth participation group. There are many ways to approach this task; none is inherently better than the rest. Whether you advertise through flyers, in the newspaper, through visits to classes in schools, or in letters to teachers, the important thing is to gather together a group

---

Sample Young Adult Library Advisory Board (YALAB) Long-Range Goals
1. To establish, throughout our library system, recognition of Young Adults as a great human resource.
2. To create a series of programs and services that will serve area teens, as well as other patron groups.
3. To be a prototype for system-wide YALAB groups. (Sprince, 1998: 248–249)

---

of teens from the area you serve and to begin to talk to them about what the library can do to better serve people their age.

The teens themselves should have input on the types of tasks they will be involved with, how often they will meet, and how their meetings will be structured. It may be helpful to provide ideas of what other teen library groups have done to spark discussion. But every library youth participation group should be different to reflect the unique needs and interests of its members.

YA Management Strategies

Tell the truth. In the young adult classic *The Catcher in the Rye*, Holden Caulfield's biggest criticism against adults is that they are "phonies." Young adults are incredibly sensitive to hypocrisy. Harold Kushner offers an interesting explanation of why this may be so in his book, *How Good Do We Have to Be?*

> Why hypocrisy, of all the sins to which the human soul is prone? I suspect young people react so strongly to it because it is an issue for them. They are bothered by the inconsistencies they find in themselves, brave one day and hiding behind lies the next, cruel to a friend in the morning and kind in the afternoon. [. . .] Teenagers are disproportionately upset by their parents' inconsistencies because a part of them has been hoping fervently, "By the time I get to be that age, I'll have solved the problem. I'll know who I am and what I stand for." They are more than disappointed, they are frightened when they learn from their parents' behavior that this is still an issue for adults. (Kushner, 1996: 77–78)

Although, as adults, we may not entirely know who we are and what we stand for, it is important to portray ourselves as honestly as possible with teens—even if it means admitting to our own flaws and imperfections.

Be organized. Young adults often are not. They are also tremendously busy. So it is helpful for Young Adult librarians to plan and prepare materials for programs ahead of time, remind teens of meeting dates and deadlines, and to set specific goals and help teens remain on task. See Chapter 6 for more information about planning and Chapter 8 for tips on organization and time management.

Get to know them. Although I recommend that you keep relationships with young adults on a professional level, that shouldn't prevent you from getting to know teens as individuals and from letting them know you care about them. During such an awkward transitional stage of their life, a little TLC can go a long way.

Ask their opinion. NEVER plan a program or make an important decision about Young Adult services in your library without first soliciting teen input.

Act on what they tell you. Don't disregard their opinions because you think you know better. In *The VOYA Reader* Mary K. Chelton recounts the following anecdote about YA librarian Leila Sprince:

> When I talked with Lee by phone, we chatted about a book promotion video the kids had made which shows a scene of a vampire (played by a LAB [Library Advisory Board] member) coming out of his coffin at night. Lee said that she was worried that nobody would be able to see the scene on film because the vampire was played by an African American kid wearing black arising from a black coffin in the shade of a large palm tree, but she then said, "I didn't say anything, though, because they have to figure these things out for themselves." I knew then why her program was so successful. (Chelton and Broderick, 1998: 241–242)

Give them ideas, but let them make their own decisions. Librarians are notorious for sharing and borrowing each other's ideas. Teens are no different. Although they often come up with wonderful ideas out of the clear blue, providing them with food for thought can often stimulate their creativity. Be careful not to push your own ideas on them, though. Teens may agree to go along with something they don't think will be successful in order to avoid hurting your feelings.

Tell them why. Try to give reasons for all the decisions you make on behalf of the library—especially if they are not popular with teens. Although they may not agree with you, at least they will understand the reasoning behind your actions.

Follow through. Do what you say you will do, whether this involves rewards or discipline. Don't make promises lightly, and keep track of what you've said.

Give them space. Teens need a lot of space to work alone or in small groups. It is helpful to break up portions of large group meetings into

Attitudes That Allow Parents to Better Support Their Teens' Growth

[This advice applies to adults who work with teens as well!]

1. desire to grow and change
2. willingness to look at what you're doing that is effective and what is not effective
3. accepting mistakes as opportunities to learn
4. willingness to look at and try alternatives
5. learning about unresolved issues that get in the way of your effectiveness
6. willingness to make new decisions and interpretations from childhood experiences
7. seeing beyond your own past issues so you can listen and understand your teen today
8. letting go—having faith in yourself and your kids (Nelsen and Lott, 1994: 23–24)

smaller individual or committee projects. Let them know you trust them enough not to be looking over their shoulder at every moment.

Make work fun. I used to keep a picture of myself with one of my Teen Library Council members wearing funny hats at one of the vendor exhibits at an ALA conference. It was a good reminder of what work was supposed to be all about—both for myself and the kids.

Goals and Expectations

Every now and then it's useful to step back and look at the big picture. What are we really trying to accomplish in our work with teens? Even more than providing information, education, and entertainment to young adults, our ultimate goal is to help teens become happy, successful, and well-adjusted adults.

In *Positive Discipline for Teenagers*, Jane Nelsen and Lynn Lott propose the following long-term goals for teenagers: courage, responsibility, cooperation, self-esteem, respect for self and others, success, and a sense of humor (1994: 30). What would you add to this list? It might also be interesting to consider what the teens you work with identify as their own life goals.

THE IMPORTANCE OF DISCIPLINE

George Holmes states that "it's important for a teenager to be given as much responsibility as possible as early as he or she can accept it" (1995: 108). But with that responsibility come certain expectations. And a failure to live up to those expectations should result in specific consequences. This section provides suggestions on how to set guidelines and enforce standards of behavior with teens in the library.

Establishing Guidelines

The easiest way to avoid problems with teens is to involve them in the process of creating "group norms" or standards of behavior. These can apply in a school media center, a Young Adult area in a public library, or in a teen advisory group—in any setting where young adults will be congregating regularly.

Creating group norms means talking openly and frankly about what standards of behavior are appropriate in a given situation. All members of the group (teens as well as adult facilitators) should have input into creating the group norms. Use a flip chart and invite participants to call out suggestions. (You may have to give them examples to get them started—this is a good way to make some of your own concerns known.) All suggestions should be written down without judgement. After all the ideas have been recorded, return to each one and discuss the pros and cons; then the group can vote on which standards to accept. If there are certain absolute standards (like library policies) that must be enforced, make that clear from the beginning and discuss those standards and the reasons behind them, without submitting them to a vote.

Post your group norms in a place where they will be visible to the group whenever they meet. This will remind them that they had input into the standards of behavior they agreed upon, which will make it easier to enforce those standards should the need arise.

Enforcing Standards of Behavior

Once the standards of behavior are drafted and agreed upon, it is the adults' responsibility to make sure they are enforced. Consistency is impor-tant. Failing to enforce a standard of behavior the group has agreed upon gives the impression you don't respect their decisions. It will also be more difficult to enforce other standards of behavior, should you need to.

Many librarians find the "three strikes" rule useful:

1. The first time you encounter a patron (this works with adults as well as teens) behaving inappropriately, approach him, tell him what

behavior is inappropriate, and why and ask him to stop immediately.

2. If he continues the inappropriate behavior, repeat that the behavior is inappropriate for the library and warn him that if he does
not stop, certain consequences will occur (he will be asked to leave
the library or suspended from the group, or whatever you or your
library has determined to be an appropriate response to the situation).

3. If he still continues the inappropriate behavior, follow through on
enforcing the consequence you warned him about.

This is yet another instance in which "doing what you say you will do"
is important. If you threaten to take action if the inappropriate behavior doesn't stop and do not do so, you will lose all credibility with the
misbehaving patron. This will also make it more difficult to enforce other
standards in the future.

Some educators use a variation on the three strikes rule that goes
something like this:

Engage the student by saying,
1. "Right now you are . . ." (describe the inappropriate behavior).
2. "I need you to . . ." (describe the preferred behavior).
3. "Can you do that?" (NOT "Will you do that?" which leaves more
room for defiance).
4. "Thank you."

This method has the advantage of getting the student's implied consent, although it doesn't necessarily provide reasons for the request. Of
course, savvy YA librarians and media specialists can combine these techniques to create a system that works best for their situation.

Troubleshooting

Even with clear expectations that are consistently enforced, there will
be times when you encounter trouble. There will be disagreements, misunderstandings, and hurt feelings. When these things happen, it may be
helpful to use many of the communication strategies in Chapter 1. Here
are some additional tips that experts have developed specifically for working with teenagers:

USING COOPERATIVE PROBLEM SOLVING

Step One: Present the problem—for example, "We keep getting
sidetracked during our Teen Advisory Board meetings and we
never get anything accomplished."

Step Two: Look for agreements that lead to solutions—"Do we all want to accomplish something at these meetings?" "Is establishing library programs and services for teens more important than the topics we wind up digressing about?"

Step Three: Gather information on the perceptions of everyone concerned—"Does everyone agree that we are digressing too much, or should we allow more time for socializing?"

Step Four: Stick to the issue and listen—"Are there any other opinions that haven't been expressed?"

Step Five: Keep asking, "Is there anything else?"

Step Six: Reflect your understanding—"What I'm hearing is that although we want to have some time to talk about our personal lives, the primary reason we are here is to accomplish library business, and we all feel frustrated if we don't get that accomplished."

Step Seven: Share your perceptions—"Although I enjoy getting to know each one of you on a personal basis, I rely on your input to help create successful Young Adult services in this library."

Step Eight: Ask your teens to reflect their understanding—"Can someone summarize our priorities for me?"

Step Nine: Brainstorm for solutions—"So, how can we balance our desire for social interaction with the need to accomplish library work? Set aside 30 minutes for socializing before the meeting? Have a break halfway through the meeting, during which people can snack and chat? Have a check-in time at the beginning of each meeting for people to talk about what's going on in their lives?"

Step Ten: Agree on a solution—"It sounds like most of us would like to try gathering earlier to socialize before the meeting."

Step Eleven: Set a date for evaluation—"Let's try that for the next three months and see how it works."

Step Twelve: Follow through—At the three-month point, touch base to see how people are feeling and whether the approach is working, and modify your strategy if needed.

Helping Teenagers Into Adulthood, Holmes, George. © 1995 by Praeger. Reproduced with permission of Greenwood Publishing Group, Inc., Westport, CT.

When we become frustrated with the behavior of the young adults we work with, it may be helpful to step back and examine the kinds of role models they have. In response to an article in *Simple Living* magazine, in which the author stated that children nowadays aren't learning

> **Teaching Not Punishing**
> - Set limits on your children's behavior.
> - Don't abdicate your authority.
> - Give your teenager increasing responsibility along with privileges.
> - Make your rules and expectations as explicit as possible.
> - Admit your mistakes. (Kutner 1997: 40–42)

values, skills, and self-discipline, Michael Fogler responds, "Oh but they are! The question is—which values are they learning? . . . I believe that if parents and society can change the values we put forth, then the children will follow suit. In fact, that's exactly what they're doing right now. When we see what our children are doing and how they are acting, we're merely looking in the mirror" (Fogler, 2000: 4).

Therefore, if library staff approach teens with hostility, suspicion, and mistrust, it should not surprise us if they treat us with a similar lack of respect. However, if we are willing to give young adults the benefit of the doubt, to "err up" in our interactions with them, and respect them as individuals, more likely than not, they will show us the same courtesy.

REFERENCES

Chelton, Mary K., and Dorothy M. Broderick, eds. 1998. *VOYA Reader Two*. Lanham, Md.: Scarecrow Press.

Covey, Stephen R. 1989. *The 7 Habits of Highly Effective People: Restoring the Character Ethic*. New York: Simon & Schuster.

Fenwick, Elizabeth, and Tony Smith. 1996. *Adolescence: The Survival Guide for Parents and Teenagers*. New York: Dorling Kindersley.

Fogler, Michael. 2000. "We're Modeling Our Values" [letter to the editor]. *Simple Living* 4 (Autumn).

Holmes, George. 1995. *Helping Teenagers Into Adulthood*. Westport, Conn.: Praeger.

Kushner, Harold S. 1996. *How Good Do We Have to Be?: A New Understanding of Guilt and Forgiveness*. Boston: Little, Brown.

Kutner, Lawrence. 1997. *Making Sense of Your Teenager*. New York: William Morrow.

Nelsen, Jane, and Lynn Lott. 1994. *Positive Discipline for Teenagers: Resolving Conflict with Your Teenage Son or Daughter*. Rocklin, Calif.: Prima.

Ponton, Lynne E. 1997. *The Romance of Risk: Why Teenagers Do the Things They Do*. New York: HarperCollins.

Shapiro, Lillian L. 1997. "Equals or Enemies?: Librarians and Young Adults." In *School Library Journal's Best: A Reader for Children's, Young Adult, and School Librarians*. Edited by Lillian N. Gerhardt. Compiled by Marilyn L. Miller and Thomas W. Downen. New York: Neal-Schuman.

Siegler, Ava L. 1997. *The Essential Guide to the New Adolescence: How to Raise an Emotionally Healthy Teenager*. New York: Penguin, Plume.

Sprince, Leila J. 1998. "For Young Adults Only—From Teen Volunteers to Young Adult Library Advisory Boards: North Regional/Broward Community College Library." In *VOYA Reader Two*. Edited by Mary K. Chelton and Dorothy M. Broderick. Lanham, Md.: Scarecrow Press.

Tapscott, Don. 1998. *Growing Up Digital: The Rise of the Net Generation*. New York: McGraw-Hill.

Young Adult Library Services Association. "YALSA Mailing Lists and Web Sites." www.ala.org/yalsa/professional/yalsalists.html (4 July 2001)

Chapter 3

Managing Staff, Teachers, and Volunteers

STAFF VS. VOLUNTEERS

No longer are volunteers expected to show up sporadically and do mundane, repetitive, behind-the-scenes tasks. The trend has been towards treating and viewing volunteers as "unpaid staff" who are subject to the benefits and expectations of other employees. The most successful volunteer programs are structured similarly to staff employment programs—which include job descriptions, interviews, orientation, training, continuing education opportunities, volunteer appreciation activities, and even evaluations (which may take the form of informal conversations to discuss the volunteers' "fit" with the job(s) assigned to them).

Keep in mind, however, that volunteers are not motivated by money (since they are not receiving any for the tasks they do in your organization). Therefore, it is important to determine what does motivate them and to make sure they receive enough of it! Although specific motivations may vary according to the individual, as early as 1976 Elfrieda McCauley wrote of school library volunteers, "Generally, they are mature, reliable, outgoing. They will want jobs not too overwhelming, not too pressing. They will look for the taste of success in the jobs they do and the joy of a job completed. They will want to feel it's a meaningful job, one worth doing. And to get credit for having a brain!" (1997: 368).

Volunteers should have access to the tools they need to get their tasks accomplished, which include a workspace and equipment. Records should be kept of volunteer time and activities. As McCauley states, "Remember that volunteers are auxiliary staff. They provide the extras: paid staff provide the essential services" (1997: 369). She also recommends that all volunteers be supervised by professional staff and not be used to replace them. This issue may be particularly important to consider if your library staff is organized. Many labor unions have guidelines on appropriate tasks for volunteers.

In spite of the unique characteristics of volunteers, most of the topics addressed in this chapter can apply to paid and volunteer staff alike.

HIRING

If your library doesn't have access to a personnel department (either in-house or through the school, city, or county with which you are affiliated), it is imperative to become familiar with the Equal Employment Act and Fair Labor Standards laws including those that relate to the Americans with Disabilities Act. Any current, reputable book on hiring staff will provide guidelines on issues to consider before you begin the hiring process. Generally accepted practices are to screen all candidates based on the same objective criteria and to ask all candidates the same interview questions, which should relate directly to their ability to do the job in question.

Recruitment

The recruitment process should involve two components—determining what you want in a candidate and attracting that candidate to your institution.

WHAT TO LOOK FOR

When seeking to hire a Young Adult librarian or media specialist, you will most likely be looking for a combination of education, experience, and less-easily defined personality traits that indicate that the candidate would work well with teens (and other adults!).

Even though a master's degree in library science is still recommended or required for professional positions in many public libraries and schools, the increasing shortage of librarians—particularly youth services librarians—may force us to reconsider these rigid educational requirements. The MLS guarantees that an individual has been exposed to, and understands, many basic library principles, but it is no guarantee of skill or ability. Furthermore, there are many bright individuals (some with a background in other areas of youth service) who would be capable of "learning the ropes" of Young Adult services on the job. Previous work experience in a library or school media center is another indicator of familiarity with library processes, but still does not guarantee the quality of a person's work.

Ideally, the combination of a written application, cover letter, resumé, and interview in addition to the testimony of references (which should be solicited from recent employers as well as individuals the candidate suggests you contact) will give you a good picture of the candidate's skills, interests, and personality.

A handful of states and national organizations have developed standards or competencies for Young Adult services, which may provide a good measuring stick for hiring decisions. One example is "Young Adults Deserve the Best," the Young Adult Library Services Association (YALSA) Competencies for Librarians Serving Youth available at www.ala.org/yalsainfo/competencies.html.

How to Find the Right Person

In the classic career guide *What Color is Your Parachute?*, Richard Nelson Bolles recommends telling everyone you know that you are looking for a job. The same goes when you are looking to hire someone for a job. Take advantage of local and national library and educational publications and the newspaper to advertise. Post your vacancy on library-related electronic discussion lists and online job services as well. Don't forget to advertise in local (and even out-of-state) library schools. Many recent (and not-so-recent) MLS graduates will be willing to move if it means landing the library job of their dreams.

Pay attention to your state association salary recommendations (which are printed in the "Career Leads" section in each issue of *American Libraries*) and make sure that your pay is competitive. Even if your library budget is tight, paying staff fairly should be a top priority. (See Chapter 7 for strategies on convincing administrators to allow you to do this.) Also, be sure to highlight other, nonmonetary perks that your library has to offer, like a competitive benefits package, award-winning library services, or unique local attractions. Successful candidates may be willing to accept a little less money to have other perks and benefits that are important to them.

Job Descriptions

When you are hiring new staff, either when filling a vacant position or creating a new one, it is a good time to examine all your department job descriptions to see if responsibilities are being distributed fairly. One way to do this is to have staff list their duties (from memory) in order of importance and to compare this list to the job description; then compare all the job descriptions to each other and adjust accordingly.

A job description should distinguish between essential and nonessential functions and address customer service as well as technical skills. There should also be some distinction between professional and para-professional duties, which should correspond to classification and pay.

Yvette Johnson maintains that job descriptions are important for a number of reasons, "They not only clarify the responsibilities of each position in the library and delineate the relationship between positions, but they also serve as the basis for the performance evaluation." She goes on to say, "An accurately written job description can be protection against litigation, because one of the factors that is used to determine if a particular work function is essential is that it is so stated in a written job description" (1995: 63,70).

TRAINING

Most libraries expect employees to come to them with a certain set of skills that qualifies them to do the job in question. Investing time in acquainting new hires with the particular details of your library system and their unique role in that institution is nonetheless a good investment. Continuing professional guidance and mentoring can make the difference between merely hiring good people and being able to maintain them for the long term.

Orientation

Orientation is a process that is designed to acquaint new employees with the library and its policies and to help them become productive members of the team as soon as possible. It is a planned effort that fosters and enhances the learning of job-related behavior. Through orientation new employees become familiar with the work setting, supervisors, co-workers, organizational values, expectations, corporate structure, and the formal employee-employer exchange relationship. (Staerkel: 1995: 83)

Although we normally think of new-employee orientation as occurring on the first day on the job, it is actually a process that begins on the first day and may continue for months, until the new employee feels comfortable and familiar with the organization and her job. This process may take longer for some employees than others and it is the job of the manager to ensure that it proceeds smoothly.

Involve YA department or media center staff in the creation of the orientation program and timeline so they can draw on their own experiences in determining what is most important to know as a new employee.

Figure 3–1
Sample New Employee Orientation Timeline

Day 1
❑ Morning—tour and New Employee Orientation Checklist with Assistant Director.
❑ Lunch—with Assistant Director and Young Adult Department Supervisor.
❑ Early afternoon—county paperwork.
❑ Late afternoon—New Employee Orientation Checklist with Young Adult Department Supervisor.

First week
❑ Complete Young Adult Department Supervisor orientation.
❑ Begin training in Young Adult Department using YA Training Checklist and YA Standard Operating Procedures (SOP) manual (paired up with staff members who are scheduled to train).
❑ Meet with Director to review Library Policy manual.
❑ Meet with Union Representative to review the union contract.
❑ Meet with Emergency Procedures Committee member to review the Emergency Procedures manual.

Second week
❑ Continue YA training using YA Training Checklist and YA SOP manual (paired up with staff members who are scheduled to train).
❑ Work with YA Department Supervisor to plan programming.

Third week
❑ Attend Young Adult Advisory Board meeting.
❑ Attend media specialists meeting—begin networking with schools.
❑ Begin collection development.
❑ Get key to library from Administrative Assistant.

Adapted with permission from the Missoula (MT) Public Library "New Employee Orientation Timeline" 2000

Remember to cover administrative and philosophical issues as well as specific job responsibilities. In her excellent essay, "On Planning and Presenting New Staff Orientations," Kathleen Staerkel provides a "Training Needs Identifier" that can also help managers determine specific areas in which the new employee may need additional training (1995: 83–102).

Orientation is as much about being introduced to people as it is about

Figure 3–2
Sample New Employee Orientation Checklist

Employee: _____   Date: _____

_____ Policy manual

_____ Union contract

_____ Standard Operating Procedures (for appropriate department)

_____ Emergency procedures and manual

_____ Chain of command (charts)

_____ Evaluation (sample form and schedule)

_____ Calendar and time sheets

_____ Friday meetings

_____ Dress code/jeans day

_____ Requesting time off

_____ Calling in sick

_____ Comp time and overtime

_____ Breaks, lunch, etc.

_____ Leaving work areas

_____ Using the library when we're closed

_____ Dynix/Internet e-mail

Dynix login (up to 9 letters/characters): _____

Dynix password (up to 9 letters/characters): _____

Internet login (up to 8 letters/characters): _____

(your address)

Internet password (up to 8 letters/characters): _____

_____ Communication (e-mail, meeting minutes, mailboxes)

_____ Off-desk time/committee work/cross-training

_____ Name tags/locker/mailbox/keys/parking sticker

_____ Intellectual Freedom/confidentiality law

_____ Priority of tasks/respect for others' work styles

_____ Flexibility (and support from management)

_____ Responsibility (on time, etc.)

_____ Open door policy

Supervisor conducting orientation: _____

Adapted with permission from the Missoula (MT) Public Library "New Employee Orientation Timeline" October, 1999 policies, procedures, and place. Therefore, it is a good idea to include all members of the department in the orientation process. Partnering the new employee with a different person every day for the first week of work can provide him with an understanding of the interrelationships of staff, as well as allow him the opportunity to get to know his colleagues. In most libraries it is traditional for the supervisor to take the new employee out for lunch on his first day of work. This allows the employee and supervisor to get to know each other better on a personal basis, as well as provides the new employee a much-needed break on what otherwise can be a very stressful day.

At the end of the orientation period, meet with the new staff member to make sure he fully understands his role within the organization and to give him feedback on his early work performance. It also makes sense to evaluate the orientation process at this point, either informally or by asking the new employee to complete an Orientation Evaluation form (a sample of which is also included in Staerkel, 1995: 100).

Work Assignments

> People require clear assignments. . . . But the responsibility for developing the work plan, the job description, and the assignment should always be on the people who do the work. (Drucker, 1990: 182)

The job description should be viewed as a framework within which employees will accomplish larger goals. Although new-employee orientation provides an introduction to the institution and the particular tasks of the job, it will ultimately be up to the individual employee to determine how she will accomplish her responsibilities. Often, new employees will bring new ideas, and their jobs will grow and evolve to accommodate them. Drucker states that the supervisor "must work both with employed staff and with volunteers so that they can think through their contribution, spell it out clearly, and evolve by joint discussion a specific work plan, with specific goals and specific deadlines" (1990: 182).

Even if work assignments allow staff members the freedom and creativity to pursue their own interests, these assignments also imply a responsibility for staff to take charge of the projects they create. The manager's role is to ensure that employees follow through on their goals and objectives.

Empowerment

In her article on "Establishing Staff Relations," Kathy Toon defines empowerment as, "let[ting] employees use their own judgement, skills and

Figure 3–3
Are You Empowering or Disempowering Your Employees?

Are You Empowering Your Employees?	Are You Disempowering Your Employees?
Do you:	*Do you:*
• Provide opportunities for employees to participate in developing goals?	• Give one-way directives?
• Provide positive rein-forcement?	• Criticize ideas?
• Show interest in their career development?	• Take back their authority?
• Listen?	• Second-guess their actions and decisions?
• Allow employees to suggest different ways of doing work?	• Do all the talking and never listen?
• Delegate responsibility *and* authority?	• Give inconsistent messages?
• Clearly define their roles and your expectations?	• Not allow their input and participation?
• Set high standards?	• Give them a job *and* the how to's?
• Demonstrate that you trust them?	• Give them a job and let them do it and then tell them it's wrong?
• Coach?	• Provide only negative feed-back?
• Ask for their help?	• Give them a job and then take it back?
• Develop their skills?	• Discourage your employees from interacting with other departments?
• Provide specific feedback?	• Express unclear goals?
• Listen to problems and help?	• Just assume people know what you want?
• Encourage learning from mistakes?	• Constantly look over your employees' shoulders?
	• Do everything yourself?
	• Advocate status quo vs. change?

(McDermott, 1992: 101) From, CAUGHT IN THE MIDDLE by Lynda D. McDermott copyright © 1992. Reprinted with permission of Prentice Hall Direct/Learning Network Direct, a part of the Learning Network.

information to make decisions" (1995: 146). This implies a shift in perspective from expecting employees to follow the rules to trusting employees to make the best decisions possible in response to specific situations within the framework of your organization's values and mission. Rules should not be so hard-and-fast that they don't allow for flexibility in extraordinary circumstances, and empowered staff understand that they will have the support of management if they make a decision to bend a rule based on a particular situation.

For example, although the Missoula Public Library in Montana does not allow patrons to volunteer at the library in lieu of paying fees for lost materials, when a teenager who had no parental support nor any form of employment lost a library book, library staff made an agreement with her social worker to allow her to bring in a letter certifying that she had completed a mutually-agreed-upon number of community service hours to "pay back" what she owed to the library and restore her borrowing privileges.

Continuing Education

Many major corporations set aside 5 percent of their personnel budgets for staff development and continuing education. If libraries and schools were able to set aside even 1 percent of their overall budgets, it would make a big difference. The staff are the greatest asset of any organization, and money spent on developing their capabilities is always well spent.

While supervisors are generally responsible for suggesting or providing continuing education opportunities, librarians themselves are in the best position to determine what kind of training they need. They can assess this through a variety of methods:

- topics of personal interest
- comparison of their knowledge and skills against their colleagues'
- performance evaluations that identify areas for improvement
- state and national lists of competencies
- changes in technology that require new knowledge
- patron requests/feedback
- long-term goals
- career aspirations
- ideas gleaned from electronic discussion lists and conferences

When several staff members express interest in the same areas of continuing education, or if the supervisor identifies a need within the de-

YALSA has trained a corps of members who are qualified to conduct staff training programs in Young Adult services throughout the
United States. Information on this program, called "Serving the
Underserved," as well as a list of qualified trainers by name or location is available at www.ala.org/yalsa/professional/trainersmain.html.
YALSA has also served as consultant on a YA training video that
was written, hosted, and produced by Michael Cart. It can be purchased through the North State Cooperative Library System, 259
North Villa Avenue, Willows, CA 95988; phone: (530) 934–2173;
fax: (530) 934–7156.

partment, there are several methods for providing staff with the information they need:

- in-service training conducted by a staff member
- in-service training conducted by a professional trainer
- in-service training conducted by a librarian from the state library
  or another school or library system
- state or national conference programs
- self-paced online courses
- video or audio training
- staff development retreats

Supervisors should also make staff aware of educational opportunities within the community such as:

- relevant courses at community colleges or universities
- programs sponsored by youth-serving agencies
- conferences and seminars conducted by national training organizations in local venues (such as Fred Pryor Seminars, National
  Seminars Group, Careertrack, and Compumaster)

At the Missoula Public Library, I did this by maintaining a three-ring
binder containing plastic protector pages in which I placed all the promotional materials we received for continuing education opportunities.
Staff were encouraged to browse the binders regularly and to notify their
supervisor if there were a training session they were interested in attending.

As Carolyn L. Cain points out in her article on "Media Specialists and
the Quest for Lifelong Learning," it is important to address not only

Figure 3–4
The Basic Principles of Personal Accountability

Blaming someone or something for your condition may be accurate, but dwelling on it will rarely help, and can even lead you away from the best solution.

More growth comes from the question, "What can I do?" than could ever come from the statement, "That's not my job."

Personal accountability is an act of courage, because to take responsibility is to take the risk of failing.

Accepting responsibility usually increases energy, intensity and focus.

At the end of our lives we remember relationships, contributions, and accomplishment. All three are acts of accountability.

Personal accountability is about making choices. The better our choices, the richer and more rewarding our lives.

Making choices is the only true way we have to express the one thing which is most precious to us: our freedom.

Basic accountability involves doing what needs to be done. Advanced accountability means taking responsibility for learning those things which will make us more effective, *and* allow us to see new opportunities to apply the principles of accountability.

From: Arnold, James K. and Stephen C. Lundin. *Personal Accountability: Your Path to a Rewarding Work Life*. Minneapolis: ChartHouse International Learning Corporation.

"learning needs that are necessary to keep current in the field—those that will help upgrade or improve our current skills and knowledge," but also, "those that are part of our basic philosophy and understanding of the mission of the profession"(1997: 155). It should not be assumed that the attainment of an MLS guarantees a complete and permanent understanding of the theoretical issues in the field. Continuing education should be encouraged as lifelong career training for Young Adult librarians and media specialists.

PERSONAL ACCOUNTABILITY

In Victor Frankl's moving account of his experiences as a Holocaust survivor, *Man's Search for Meaning*, he places emphasis on the fundamental choice that an individual always has, regardless of his circumstances, to choose the attitude with which he will respond to any given situation. Taking advantage of that freedom of choice is what Lundin and Arnold refer to as "personal accountability" (1959).

The most successful staff members do this intuitively; others may need to be taught how to choose deliberate responses and appropriate actions in lieu of following the whims of their moods. Jennifer Carter, a business trainer and motivational speaker based in Missoula, Montana, suggests thinking of your job as "being on stage" and recommends leaving your personal problems at home, or at the very least, in the car, when you arrive at work. As soon as you walk through the door into the library, she suggests you don your professional persona and leave it intact until you leave the building at the end of the day.

This means treating colleagues with the same respect and consideration that you would patrons. The notion of personal accountability is particularly relevant with teenagers, who often tend to "push our buttons" by directly addressing weaknesses that adults would generally be more tactful in avoiding. Remembering that our response to these attacks (and other difficult situations) is entirely in our control can be empowering.

FOSTERING TEAMWORK

Teaching staff to be personally accountable for their actions and responses to situations does not preclude the possibility of working in teams. In fact, people who assume responsibility for their own decisions make excellent team members.

Managers can help foster teamwork by encouraging staff members to see their role in the organization as a part of a larger whole. What follows are a few specific strategies to help staff learn to work better together.

Cross-Training

One way to help staff better understand and appreciate each other's roles is to rotate duties within the department. For example, staff could take turns having primary responsibility for coordinating the Teen Advisory Board, selecting certain types of materials, or planning particular programs.

If you determine that specialization is important in your department, you can still temporarily partner staff members with each other to walk them through the steps of each other's jobs in order for them to gain a

Figure 3–5
Strategies for Improving the Internal Facilitator's Role

1. Clarify personal interests regarding the role of the facilitator.
2. Anticipate and discuss role conflicts before the conflicts arise.
3. Create opportunities to educate others about the facilitator's role.
4. Become identified with different groups in the organization rather than one particular group.
5. Clarify when one is switching roles.
6. Use the core values in one's nonfacilitator role.
7. Discuss problems in past working relationships with potential client groups.
8. Turn down facilitator assignments when it is impossible to be substantively neutral.
9. Be willing to give up the facilitator role.
10. Become an informal internal organizational change agent.

Schwartz, Roger M. © 1994. *The Skilled Facilitator: Practical Wisdom for Developing Effective Groups.* San Francisco: Jossey-Bass Inc., 238. Reprinted by permission of Jossey-Bass a subsidiary of John Wiley & sons, Inc.

better understanding of the interdependence of all functions of the department.

Committees and Task Forces

We've all heard the groans that usually meet any suggestion of forming a committee or task force in the library. I believe that is because many committees and task forces are conducted inefficiently and drag on for too long. If conducted properly, committees are an ideal way to address issues that affect the whole department, or even several departments in the public library, or the whole school.

The key to having an effective committee is to assign an organized and effective facilitator who is capable of delegating work assignments to committee members. This need not be a supervisor (and the group may actually have more success if it is led by someone who is considered to be a peer), but facilitators should have some training in how to conduct an effective meeting. (For more guidelines on conducting meetings refer to "Group Meetings" in the next section.)

Schwartz points out that the "challenge for the facilitator is to help role-set constituents think in terms of roles and to explain that while serving as a facilitator, she cannot engage in nonfacilitator role behaviors that conflict with the facilitator role" (1994: 235). In other words, the per-

> **maieutic,** *adj.* relating to or resembling the Socratic method of elic-
> iting new ideas from another (*Merriam-Webster's 365 New Words
> Calendar*)

son responsible for YA collection development should not use her role
as facilitator of the budgeting committee in order to get more money to
purchase materials for the Young Adult collection. The facilitator must
remain neutral.

MEETINGS

Meetings can take many forms. They can be a one-on-one interaction
between a supervisor and a subordinate, a gathering of the Young Adult
services department or school media staff, or a get-together of teens to
brainstorm ideas. Meetings are convened to gather information, provide
feedback, and generate ideas. They may occur on a regular basis or be
called to address particular issues. Although the particulars of a meeting will vary depending on the situation, here are a few general guidelines it may be useful to follow.

Formal vs. Informal

Although we often think of meetings as scheduled events, with an agenda
and minutes, or a planned conversation between two individuals, effective managers also take advantage of impromptu meetings. Many business management specialists recommend "management by walking
around," a process in which supervisors are encouraged to get out of their
offices periodically to casually check in with their employees and see how
things are going. This is an easy form of management for many Young
Adult librarians and school media specialists since we are likely to work
side-by-side with our staff members in many circumstances.

Informal group meetings can also be held by catching a group of
people you need to talk to for a brief chat or calling together department members for a few minutes at the beginning or end of the day to
share any relevant information that may have come up. Kathy Toon recounts the story of a branch library in which "the manager held informal staff meetings each morning by calling all of the staff to the break
room for a coffee break about fifteen minutes before the library opened"
(1995: 145). When using such "breaks" to conduct business, however, it
should be clear to the staff that they will get paid for their time.

All coaching processes take place with one of two goals in mind: to *solve problems* or to *improve performance.*

Individual Meetings

Pam Barry is my role model for providing individualized attention to staff. When she was director of Youth Services at the Carmel Clay Public Library in Indiana, she would meet with each full-time staff member monthly (and with part-time staff every six weeks) as well as conduct monthly staff (group) meetings. This guaranteed each employee an hour of uninterrupted time to discuss her progress, ask questions, and seek input from her supervisor. It provided the supervisor the opportunity to provide guidance and regular feedback to each staff member so the annual performance evaluation never came as a surprise.

Scheduled individual meetings can be a useful tool for coaching and exchanging information, but they should not provide an excuse for a supervisor to put off discussion of unpleasant issues that need to be addressed immediately. Disciplinary actions should always occur as soon as possible after an incident (and behind closed doors).

Group Meetings

Like individual meetings, group meetings can also be held on a regular basis (such as a monthly staff meeting) to exchange information or in response to a particular situation. Mary Fellows suggests that any of the following may be accomplished in a group meeting:

- provide information
- gather input or data
- train
- inspire
- plan
- solve problems
- resolve conflict
- set goals
- evaluate progress towards goals (1995: 134)

Regardless of purpose, most effective meetings share the following characteristics:

Planning the meeting: Determine where the meeting will be held. Factors to consider are how many people will attend, who the players are, and what type of atmosphere you want to convey. (Meetings that take place in the staff lounge may have a more informal feel than those that take place in the supervisor's office, for example.) Make sure the room is arranged so everyone can see each other and that all potential distractions (such as ringing phones) have been addressed.

Agenda: An agenda can be drawn up by the supervisor and posted in the department or delivered to staff members several days before the meeting. When using this model, staff members are asked to get agenda items to the supervisor well in advance of the meeting. An alternative is to post a blank agenda in the media center or YA department where staff members can write agenda items as they come to mind. The supervisor will still want to review the items (to determine whether some of them might be more appropriately addressed on an individual basis) and add his own before considering the agenda to be final.

Set time frame: The time the meeting is scheduled for should be clearly stated. Meetings should begin on time regardless of whether all staff members are present—waiting for absent staff members before beginning a meeting only sends the message that there is no reason to arrive promptly. Since attention generally begins to wane after approximately 90 minutes, I recommend not scheduling a meeting that will last longer than that.

Introduction: The supervisor should welcome staff to the meeting and review the agenda items, noting approximately how much time should be spent on each item. It will be the job of the supervisor to make sure each item gets discussed in the allotted amount of time. If this proves to be impossible, a committee may be assigned to examine the issue in more detail, or discussion may continue at a follow-up meeting. In most cases, discussion of one agenda item should not be allowed to continue at the expense of running out of time to discuss other items on the meeting agenda.

Agenda items: Agenda items should be presented in the meeting by those they pertain to. For example, a Young Adult department meeting may include a report on Teen Advisory Board activities from the librarian who coordinates that group, as well as an update on summer reading planning from a spokesperson on that committee.

Figure 3–6
Ground Rules for Effective Groups

1. Test assumptions and inferences.
2. Share all relevant information.
3. Focus on interests, not positions.
4. Be specific—use examples.
5. Agree on what important words mean.
6. Explain the reasons behind one's statements, questions, and actions.
7. Disagree openly with any member of the group.
8. Make statements, then invite questions and comments.
9. Jointly design ways to test disagreements and solutions.
10. Discuss undiscussable issues.
11. Keep the discussion focused.
12. Do not take cheap shots or otherwise distract the group.
13. All members are expected to participate in all phases of the process.
14. Exchange relevant information with nongroup members.
15. Make decisions by concensus.
16. Do self-critiques.

Developing Effective Groups. San Francisco: Jossey-Bass Inc.: 75. Reprinted by permission of Jossey-Bass a subsidary of John Wiley & Sons, Inc.

Troubleshooting: Personality conflicts and communication problems are some of the most common problems that occur in group meetings. *Getting Past No: Negotiating with Difficult People* by William Ury and *Dealing with People You Can't Stand: How to Bring Out the Best in People at Their Worst* by Rick Brinkman and Rick Kirschner are two good sources of strategies for dealing with specific personality and communication issues. As Schwartz reminds us, "group facilitation is not therapy. The purpose of dealing with emotions that arise in group facilitation is to help the group become more effective at its work, not to change people's personalities or to focus on emotions for their own sake. To be appropriate, the facilitator's interventions on members' emotional behaviors must relate to the group's effectiveness"(1994: 191).

Ending the meeting: If staff were allowed sufficient input in the creation of the meeting agenda, there shouldn't be a need for an "other business" category at the end of the meeting. However, allot a few extra minutes at the end of the meeting for items that anyone forgot to plan for, as well as for questions and follow-up to unresolved agenda items.

Minutes: The supervisor or facilitator should type up minutes to the meeting as soon as possible. (Laptops and PDAs may actually allow librarians to create the minutes during the meeting itself.) Minutes should include a summary of all discussion as well as a record of any follow-up action to be taken, with the name of the person or people responsible for such action.

Evaluation/Follow-up: Managers should take a few minutes at the end of each meeting to assess the climate of the meeting. They may want to solicit feedback from others who attended as well. If there were any problems in the way the meeting was conducted, a strategy should be developed for addressing those problems in future meetings. The supervisor or facilitator should also make a note of any unfinished business, which should be followed up at the next meeting.

PERFORMANCE EVALUATIONS

As mentioned earlier, if regular formal and informal meetings are conducted with staff throughout the year, the annual performance evaluation should not be difficult for the supervisor or hold any surprises for the employee. Although performance evaluations take many forms, they should always address clear, concrete, and measurable goals. As Marie Orlando states in her essay "Staff Evaluation," "If you work with a plan including a schedule of goals and objectives to be completed, then it becomes almost formulaic to determine whether each member of your department 'team' is contributing to their achievement" (1995: 116).

State and national competencies again provide good measuring sticks for acceptable performance in the areas of Young Adult services. Areas for improvement should be conveyed as learning opportunities rather than criticisms, and the employee should always be asked if she needs any additional tools or training to accomplish her goals.

Self-Evaluation

Asking employees to rate their own job performance may provide them with a greater sense of control over what otherwise can be a stressful process. Self-evaluation also provides insights into what the individual perceives as her own areas of weakness and achievement. A self-rating performance evaluation form should provide the opportunity for the supervisor to discuss the staff member's performance as well. Make clear to the employee, however, that the objective is not for her to accurately guess what the supervisor's rating will be, but rather to represent a subjective and (hopefully more) balanced evaluation of job performance.

Documenting Performance

As stated earlier, negative feedback should not be "held back" until the performance evaluation, but should be given immediately to address specific incidents as they occur. Records should be kept of these incidents, however. Records may range from an informal notation for a verbal warning, to a copy of a memorandum or written warning or any correspondence with higher-level supervisors regarding problem behavior. Keep in mind that these records may be viewed by others (in the case of a grievance or lawsuit), so stick to the facts and be professional in your language and approach. Similar records should be kept to document achievements and exceptionally good performance. These records should be reviewed at the time of the performance evaluation and addressed in that document as well. Keeping this type of portfolio on each employee serves a dual purpose of jogging the memory at the time of the annual review as well as creating a paper trail should any further disciplinary action become necessary.

Feedback from Staff?

Peter Drucker recommends asking every one with whom you work, "What am I doing that helps you with your work? What am I doing that hampers you?" (1990: 184). In addition to this type of informal conversations throughout the year, you might want to offer employees the opportunity to evaluate your work as a supervisor. Although the idea may seem intimidating, no one (other than you) needs to see these evaluations, and they may provide employees with a nonthreatening way to offer you good suggestions.

Caution should be taken not to associate these reviews in any way with the employee performance evaluation, however. In fact, the best time to request feedback from your employees might be a month or two after their performance evaluation—when they are less likely to respond with a knee-jerk reaction to their own job appraisal and their next evaluation is far enough off that they won't fear retribution. Another way to approach this is to invite all your employees to evaluate your performance at the same time each year. They may be more likely to respond honestly if you offer them the option of submitting their evaluation anonymously. Supervisor evaluations should also be voluntary.

DISCIPLINE AND TROUBLESHOOTING

Perhaps the most unpleasant job of a manager is to confront and/or discipline staff for inappropriate behavior. This task is so unpleasant that many of us avoid it as much as possible. However, it is best to deal with difficult situations directly and as soon as possible after the incident occurs. A few strategies can help make this job a little easier.

Addressing Issues Before They Become Problems

The primary reason for addressing issues as quickly as possible is to prevent them from escalating further. Lack of action by the manager implies consent. Therefore, ignoring inappropriate behavior is never an acceptable response.

Meeting regularly with staff members on an individual basis, either in formal meetings or casual encounters, is a good way to provide both positive and negative feedback and to prevent minor issues from developing into problems. Pfeiffer offers the following guidelines for giving appropriate feedback:

1. Consider the needs of others.
2. Describe behavior only; do not attempt to interpret.
3. Focus on behavior that can be changed.
4. Be specific.
5. Wait for feedback to be solicited.
6. Be nonjudgemental.
7. Give feedback immediately after the behavior.
8. Allow the freedom to change or not to change.
9. Express feelings directly. (1994, *Group*, 25: 27–30)

All these suggestions apply to positive feedback, but the supervisor will need to use his discretion in offering negative feedback. For example, depending on the severity of the situation, allowing the freedom to change or not to change may not be an option. Negative feedback is rarely solicited, but often essential to staff growth and development.

Effective Discipline

Supervisors should be familiar with the traditional tests of "just cause" before initiating any disciplinary action. In our increasingly litigious society, just cause is what a jury or arbitrator would be looking for should the disciplinary action be challenged in court or in a grievance process. Although elements of every situation are subjective, particular guidelines are considered when determining just cause. These include:

1. Notice—Was the employee clearly informed of the possible or probable consequences of her actions?

2. Reasonable Rule or Order—Did the rule or order directly relate to a) the orderly, efficient, and safe operation of the business, and b) performance that might properly be expected of the employee?
3. Investigation—Before the disciplinary action was taken, did the supervisor verify that the employee had done something wrong?
4. Fair Investigation—Was the investigation conducted fairly and objectively?
5. Proof—Is there evidence or proof that the employee is guilty as charged?
6. Equal Treatment—Are rules, orders, and penalties applied fairly and equitably to all employees?
7. Penalty—Did the severity of the disciplinary action directly relate to the a) seriousness of the proven offense, and b) employee's prior record?

In addition to putting you on solid ground legally, the seven tests of just cause can help you determine whether you are being fair in your expectations and assessment of the problem situation. If you find that the principles of just cause don't seem to apply to your situation, perhaps you should reconsider whether to move ahead with disciplinary action and more closely examine the specifics of the situation and your own personal motives in addressing it.

Personal Problems in the Workplace

Although ideally staff members would leave their personal problems at home, we all know that work performance often suffers when staff members are having trouble in their personal lives. Supervisors may learn of these difficulties through the grapevine or from the employee who is experiencing the problem. Or they may merely suspect there are personal problems, based on an individual employee's behavior. If work performance is not affected, it is best to maintain a compassionate attitude and not directly address the situation unless the employee brings it up.

However, if work performance or relationships with staff or patrons suffer, the issue needs to be addressed directly with the employee. Discussions should focus on the specific behaviors that are interfering with the employee's ability to do his job. If the employee offers an explanation of his personal situation, try not to diagnose the problem or offer psychological counseling. If your library offers an employee assistance program or other counseling services, refer the staff member to that agency for professional help. You may also want to mention whether the library's employee benefits will cover the cost of counseling.

It will ultimately be the decision of the staff member to seek professional help with his personal problem, however. Although difficult during a time of crisis, it is important to make clear to your employee that, while you may empathize with his problem, inappropriate behavior cannot regularly be tolerated in the workplace. You may, however, decide to make temporary accommodations for extreme situations (such as divorce, major illness, or death in the family).

If an employee has repeated behavior problems as a result of an addiction or other mental or physical illness, the library may mandate counseling as a condition for continued employment. Before making such a determination, however, you will want to consult with your library's personnel department and/or attorney.

Letting People Go

When repeated disciplinary actions do not bring about the desired results, it may be necessary to dismiss or reassign an employee. Ideally, unresolvable problems would be identified during the employee's probationary period, during which no explanation is required to let an employee go. After the probationary period, it is very important to determine just cause before dismissing a staff member. As unpleasant as firing an employee can be, it is sometimes necessary and preferable to tolerating repeated instances of inappropriate behavior.

However, sometimes an employee may be having problems performing the duties of her position simply because her strengths lie in other areas. A particularly shy staff member may be more comfortable working behind the scenes, while a theatrical staff member may be better suited to booktalking and coordinating programs instead of working at a desk. When it is possible to reassign a staff member according to her skills and work preferences, this might be a better option than an outright dismissal.

STAFF APPRECIATION

Managers should show staff appreciation regularly and in a variety of ways—from providing sincere, positive feedback to hosting staff appreciation parties. At the Missoula Public Library we created a "staff appreciation" bulletin board on which anyone could post a public thank you to anyone else for a positive action. At the Carmel Clay Public Library in Indiana, youth services staff members created a "morale committee" that helped to keep spirits up during the insanely busy summer reading period by providing tasty treats and small gifts for staff mem-

> **misoneism,** *n.* hatred or dislike of what is new or represents change (The Random House College Dictionary)

bers at random times throughout the summer. Greeting cards and electronic greetings can be used to show your appreciation for an employee's exceptional work or a job well done. And departmental outings and small gifts can also show staff members that you value their contributions.

Kouzes and Posner offer the following additional suggestions for "appreciating constituents":

- Be accessible—even at home.
- Listen everywhere and listen well.
- Learn your constituents' stories.
- Step outside your cultural experience.
- Keep in touch.
- Become an employee for the day.
- Hold a regular forum with key constituencies.
- Ante up first.
- Know what "bugs" your constituents.
- Practice small wins (acknowledge small achievements). (1993: 112–118)

MANAGING CHANGE

> Those interested in perpetuating present conditions are always in tears about the marvelous past that is about to disappear, without having so much as a smile for the young future.—Attributed to Simone de Beauvoir (McDermott, 1992)

Perhaps the biggest challenge to library managers in the 21st century is the rapid pace of change. Employees can no longer learn the skills of their trade and expect to rely on those skills for their entire career. On the contrary, once a skill is mastered, more likely than not another skill needs to be developed to respond to change in a different area.

This instability can be unsettling, as illustrated in Octavia Butler's novel, *The Parable of the Sower*, in which the young protagonist in a dystopian society founds a religion of sorts whose foundation is the concept of change, since change is the only constant in her world. Resistance to change is natural. People coping with change usually experience some form of denial and resistance before moving on to curiosity and

> For more practical tips and step-by-step strategies from business and management experts on employee management, check out *The Winning Manager: Leadership Skills for Greater Innovation, Quality, and Employee Commitment* by Julius E. Eitington.

acceptance. Nonetheless, resistance to change can be frustrating for a manager who is eager to implement new and exciting ideas.

Helpful strategies for implementing change include:

- explaining why the change is necessary
- defining the outcomes and results to be achieved
- providing a positive picture of the future
- taking small steps
- understanding and planning for resistance
- developing strategies to provide new skills
- celebrating small steps towards change (adapted from McDermott, 1992: 132)

Although managing staff and volunteers can sometimes be challenging, developing a team that works well together to accomplish common goals can be one of the most rewarding aspects of library work.

REFERENCES

Arnold, James K., and Stephen C. Lundin. 1997. *Personal Accountability: Your Path to a Rewarding Work Life*. Minneapolis: Chart House International Learning Corporation

Brinkman, Rick, and Rick Kirschner. 1994. *Dealing with People You Can't Stand: How to Bring Out the Best in People at Their Worst*. New York: McGraw-Hill.

Cain, Carolyn. 1997. "Media Specialists and the Quest for Lifelong Learning." In *School Library Journal's Best: A Reader for Children's, Young Adult, and School Librarians*. Edited by Lillian N. Gerhardt; compiled by Marilyn L. Miller and Thomas W. Downen. New York: Neal-Schuman.

Covey, Stephen R. 1999. *Living the 7 Habits: Stories of Courage and Inspiration*. New York: Simon & Schuster.

Drucker, Peter F. 1990. *Managing the Non-profit Organization*. New York: HarperCollins.

Fellows, Mary. 1995. "Conducting Effective Meetings." In *Youth Ser-

vices Librarians as Managers: A How-To Guide from Budgeting to Personnel. Edited by Kathleen Staerkel, Mary Fellows, and Sue McCleaf Nespeca. Chicago: American Library Association.

Frankl, Victor E. 1959. *Man's Search for Meaning: An Introduction to Logotherapy*. New York: Washington Square Press.

Johnson, Yvette. 1995. "Job Descriptions." In *Youth Services Librarians as Managers: A How-To Guide from Budgeting to Personnel*. Edited by Kathleen Staerkel, Mary Fellows, and Sue McCleaf Nespeca. Chicago: American Library Association.

Kouzes, James M., and Barry Z. Posner. 1993. *Credibility: How Leaders Gain and Lose It, Why People Demand It*. San Francisco: Jossey-Bass.

McCauley, Elfrieda. 1997. "Volunteers? Yes!" In *School Library Journal's Best: A Reader for Children's, Young Adult, and School Librarians*. Edited by Lillian N. Gerhardt; compiled by Marilyn L. Miller and Thomas W. Downen. New York: Neal-Schuman.

McDermott, Lynda C. 1992. *Caught in the Middle: How to Survive and Thrive in Today's Management Squeeze*. Englewood Cliffs, N.J.: Prentice-Hall.

Merriam-Webster's 365 New Words Calendar. New York: Workman Publishing. Wednesday, September 6, 2000.

Orlando, Marie. 1995. "Staff Evaluation." In *Youth Services Librarians as Managers: A How-To Guide from Budgeting to Personnel*. Edited by Kathleen Staerkel, Mary Fellows, and Sue McCleaf Nespeca. Chicago: American Library Association.

Pfeiffer, J. William, ed. 1994. "The Coaching Process." In *Theories and Models in Applied Behavioral Science: Group, 25*. San Diego: Pfeiffer & Company.

Pfeiffer, J. William, ed. 1994. "The Coaching Process." In *Theories and Models in Applied Behavioral Science: Group, 26*. San Diego: Pfeiffer & Company.

The Random House College Dictionary. 1984. New York: Random House.

Schwartz, Roger M. 1994. *The Skilled Facilitator: Practical Wisdom for Developing Effective Groups*. San Francisco: Jossey-Bass.

Staerkel, Kathleen. 1995. "On Planning and Presenting New Staff Orientations." In *Youth Services Librarians as Managers: A How-To Guide from Budgeting to Personnel*. Edited by Kathleen Staerkel, Mary Fellows, and Sue McCleaf Nespeca. Chicago: American Library Association.

Toon, Kathy. 1995. "Establishing Staff Relations." In *Youth Services Li-*

brarians as Managers: A How-To Guide from Budgeting to Person-nel. Edited by Kathleen Staerkel, Mary Fellows, and Sue McCleaf Nespeca. Chicago: American Library Association.

Ury, William. 1991. *Getting Past No: Negotiating with Difficult People*. New York: Bantam Books.

Chapter 4

Managing Horizontally and Up

Here is the very heart and soul of the matter: If you look to lead, invest at least 40% of your time to managing yourself—your ethics, character, principle, purpose, motivation, and conduct. Invest at least 30% managing those with authority over you, and 15% managing your peers. Use the remainder to induce those you 'work for' to understand and practice the theory... if you don't understand that you should be working for your mislabeled 'subordinates' you haven't understood anything. Lead yourself, lead your superiors, lead your peers, and free your people to do the same. All else is trivial! (Attributed to Dee Hock, founder of VISA Card, in Levey, 1998: 103)

BOSSES

"Managing your boss" may sound like a somewhat sinister concept, but if you view management in the context I introduced in Chapter 1—as forming relationships—I think you will agree that managing your boss is important. This doesn't mean catering to your boss's every whim or sacrificing your own beliefs, but rather developing a good working relationship in which you can express your opinions and earn the respect of your supervisor. You can do this in much the same way you would earn the respect of your subordinates—by being honest, respectful, forthcoming, creative, hard-working, responsible, reliable, prompt, and efficient, and by communicating openly.

In exchange for your boss's respect, you will be expected to support her decisions. Although a good boss will seek input from middle-managers before making important decisions that will affect the library, it is important to recognize that your supervisor ultimately has the final word. And regardless of whether you agree with the decision, you will be expected to uphold it. Furthermore, you should do this with a smile on your face. In the same way you expect your staff members to enforce rules they may not agree with, your supervisor will expect you to do so, cheerfully.

If you have serious qualms about an administrative decision, it is your responsibility to make sure your supervisor understands your perspective. But once a final decision has been made, your only options are to uphold the decision or find another job (or to appeal to your supervisor's supervisor in accordance with your library's policy). This may sound severe, but it is imperative that all levels of management reinforce one another so staff don't receive a different message from their department supervisor than they do from the library director.

There is much truth behind the saying "it is lonely at the top," and good supervisors will appreciate your support and camaraderie.

COLLEAGUES

Young Adult librarians and media specialists are frequently the only adults in their departments. But even if they supervise other staff members, the hierarchical relationship may make it awkward to develop close friendships with their subordinates. Therefore, it is important to reach out to other department supervisors or teachers. Having friends who are in similar, yet different, positions within your organization can be a great way to get neutral feedback on ideas and to share perceptions of library or school-wide issues.

In addition to making work more enjoyable, building relationships with your colleagues also sets the stage for collaborative programs such as

---

In building strategic alliances successfully, you must learn how to:

- Establish up front why the alliance exists and determine mutually beneficial goals.
- Develop shared plans that outline resources and schedules.
- Avoid using formal authority to overcome resistance and gain cooperation on resolving issues.
- Appreciate and develop synergistic ways to work effectively with the diversity of operating styles and cultures brought into the alliance by the key players.
- Explore opportunities to bring others into the alliance so as to strengthen the outcomes and expand the network. (McDermott, 1992: 123)

book and movie discussions (jointly hosted by the YA and AV departments) or booktalking in the classrooms of subject teachers.

NETWORKING

Whereas teachers work in the same building with dozens of people who serve the same clientele in essentially the same ways, school media specialists and Young Adult specialists are often working in relative isolation. It is therefore important to reach beyond the walls of the library to form alliances with other Young Adult librarians, media specialists, and youth services workers.

School-Public Library Relations

One of the most important relationships should be forged between the local middle and high schools and the public library. The librarians in these institutions are doing essentially the same work (albeit with a different focus) with the same clientele.

Public librarians should attend media specialists' meetings and vice

---

Ideas for Cooperative Activities

1. informal meetings between public and school librarians
2. exchanged lists of collection holdings
3. jointly planned summer reading programs
4. joint compilation of community resources
5. joint planning of community programs
6. joint material evaluation, selection, acquisition, and processing programs
7. placement of public library book catalogs in school libraries
8. joint development of storytelling groups to improve techniques and skills
9. reciprocal borrowing and lending of materials
10. class-orientation visits to the public library
11. booktalks by public librarians given in the schools
12. curriculum guides and units of instruction provided to the public library
13. in-service programs designed around topics of mutual interest and concern
14. production facilities for materials
15. preparation of union lists or catalogs
16. access to specialized and computerized data bases
17. joint film cooperatives (Bender, 1997: 219)

If you're not sure how well you're doing on collaboration with your counterpart in the schools or public library, you can use Kay E. Vandergrift's "Self Evaluation Inventory on School-Public Library Cooperation," which was published in an article called "Cooperative Dialogue: Using an Instrument to Empower" in the *VOYA Reader Two*. (Vandergrift, 1998: 255–259)

versa. Public and school librarians should share information about assignments and resources to address assignment needs. They should cooperate to provide complementary services to each other's institutions. (For example, the YA librarian from the public library could booktalk popular fiction to middle school or high school classes and the school library media specialist could provide guidance in collection development of curricular support materials to the public library.) When roles overlap, public and school librarians can collaborate to host joint programs and provide better services.

The key to successful school/public library partnerships is clear and consistent communication. It is imperative that the Young Adult librarian and the school media specialist communicate directly and respectfully about any activities that include providing services in what might be perceived as the other's "turf." For example, the school library media specialist should be the first point of contact for a public librarian who wishes to booktalk in subject teachers' classrooms, and a media specialist should consult with the Young Adult librarian before embarking on a joint assignment alert program with the adult reference department in the public library.

Local Librarians Similar to You

Another important group of people to network with are those who do the same job you do in other institutions (Young Adult librarians in other public libraries or school library media specialists in other schools). It should be fairly easy to network with these people through your school or library system and through regional and state library associations. As recipients of the Frances Henne/YALSA/VOYA Research Grant, John P. Bradford and Sheila B. Anderson conducted research in 1999 and 2000 pertaining to state library associations for Young Adult librarians and state youth service coordinators responsible for services to young adults. The results are listed at www.ala.org/yalsa/profdev/leadership.html.

If your local library association doesn't have a division or interest group for Young Adult librarians, why not start one? Start a newsletter or listserv. Or, better yet, host a monthly meeting of Young Adult librarians in your area to share ideas. Of course, networking on the national level is another way of learning more about what other librarians like you are up to. Young Adult Library Services Association (www.ala.org/yalsa) and American Association of School Librarians (www.ala.org/aasl) are excellent places to start.

Other Youth Specialists

Young Adult librarians and media specialists often overlook other sources of information about the clients we serve. Boys and Girls Clubs, YMCAs/YWCAs, parks and recreation departments, sports organizations, churches, and other local associations (including the fire and police departments) may be able to provide valuable information about the teens in your community and their needs and interests. The library, in turn, can share resources with these organizations, for the ultimate benefit of the kids.

Other Young Adult Library Groups

Another form of networking can be done between your school or library's teen advisory group and another group within your state. YAs can get together for an afternoon, evening, or overnight (in the library) to socialize and share ideas. To network with other coordinators of Young Adult Advisory Committees (YAAC) across the nation, consider joining YALSA's YA-YAAC listserv. For information on subscribing, see Chapter 2.

ADVOCACY

Although many adolescents are intent on appearing self-sufficient, the truth is kids need adults. They need adults who are not their parents or teachers to serve as mentors and role models. And, because our society still refuses to take most teens seriously, they need adults as advocates to speak out on their behalf, to defend their interests, and, perhaps most importantly, to allow their own voices to be heard.

Listening and responding to teens in the Young Adult department or media center is only the first step. True youth advocacy means finding ways for teen voices to be heard by others as well. Often this will mean defending ideas that challenge the status quo. It may mean educating adult services and children's librarians and library administrators about the developmental tasks of young adults or fighting for more equitable enforcement of library policies. It might mean speaking to local government officials about the needs of teens in your community. And it might mean modeling by example to show others how to treat teenagers as people worth listening to.

Lynne Ponton, in her book *The Romance of Risk: Why Teenagers Do the Things They Do*, states, "Advocacy for youth has to be taught. It is a complex package of skills that include an interest in and ability to identify with youth, education about the problems facing young people and about what would make a difference, and a strong commitment to fight for individual adolescents and, on a larger scale, for the entire age group" (1997: 279).

Although defending the rights of teens can be challenging, it can also be very rewarding. And the library and community will benefit as much as the teens themselves from a system that takes into consideration the opinions of its youth.

REFERENCES

Bender, David R. 1997. "Networking and School Library Media Programs." In *School Library Journal's Best: A Reader for Children's, Young Adult, and School Librarians*. Edited by Lillian N. Gerhardt; compiled by Marilyn L. Miller and Thomas W. Downen. New York: Neal-Schuman.

Levey, Joel, and Michelle Levey. 1998. *Living in Balance: A Dynamic Approach for Creating Harmony & Wholeness in a Chaotic World*. Berkeley: Conari Press.

McDermott, Lynda C. 1992. *Caught in the Middle: How to Survive and Thrive in Today's Management Squeeze*. Englewood Cliffs, N.J.: Prentice-Hall.

Ponton, Lynne E. 1997. *The Romance of Risk: Why Teenagers Do the Things They Do*. New York: HarperCollins.

Vandergrift, Kay E. 1998. "Cooperative Dialogue: Using an Instrument to Empower." In *VOYA Reader Two*. Edited by Mary K. Chelton and Dorothy M. Broderick. Lanham, Md.: Scarecrow Press.

Part II

Administration

Chapter 5

Managing Projects: Collections, Resources, Programs, and Events

THE YA COLLECTION

Although we often talk about collection development (or the selection of materials) in libraries, we don't often consider collection management (or a more comprehensive approach to maintaining the collection). Material selection is one component of collection management, but strategic planning, weeding, and access should also be considered.

Scope

First and foremost, the scope of the Young Adult or school media collection should be clearly defined:

If you are a public library:

- Do you provide curricular support as well?
- Is Young Adult nonfiction housed in the YA or the adult collection?
- Do you have reference materials in your YA area?
- What about AV materials?

If you are a school library:

- Do you support recreational reading as well?
- Is popular fiction shelved separately from the literary works used for class assignments?
- Are you also responsible for coordinating your school's audiovisual department?

The scope of your collection should be determined with input from other departments and teachers (and teens as well), and it should be clearly conveyed and understood by library or school staff and patrons alike.

Strategic Planning

Regular assessments of the Young Adult collection should be conducted to see which items are circulating well and which are gathering dust on the shelves. An annual or semiannual inventory can also be useful in determining which titles have disappeared and may need to be replaced. Reports can also help in determining trends, such as an increase in the circulation of horror books or a decrease in the popularity of a YA magazine.

Surveys, particularly those conducted through the schools (since they allow you to gather information from a large number of students at once), can also be useful in determining teen interests for collection development. Young Adult librarians and school media specialists with popular materials collections should also keep an eye to the media and pop culture to assist them in discerning the ever changing trends of teens.

Access

Surveys and reports can also help you determine how teens use the YA collection, which should provide ideas on how to arrange the collection in order to maximize its use. For example, if your survey indicated that humor was a popular genre in your community, you might want to shelve the humor books separately or use genre stickers on the spines of the books to indicate which titles fall into that category. The same type of displays or stickers can be used to indicate popular titles (selected by local teens) in your area. It might also make sense to shelve series fiction together, rather than alphabetically by author.

Weeding

Weeding of old, unused, damaged, or inaccurate titles should be done on a regular basis (in conjunction with collection usage reports). However, librarians must also consider in-house use when weeding the collection, since some titles (such as those on teen sex) may be used in the library, but not checked out.

Teen advisory groups can help out with weeding, at least as an initial screen to recommend materials that might be candidates for discarding, with librarians making final decisions. When I implemented this strategy I was surprised to find teens were pulling paperbacks in exceptionally good condition as candidates for weeding. Their rationale was if the book still looked that good after being in the library for a while, no one must be reading it!

When space is limited, it may be difficult to maintain a core collection of YA classics as well as the latest titles. The library's mission and role priorities as well as the scope of the YA collection should provide guidance on what types of materials to emphasize. Consideration should also be given to what kinds of YA materials are available in other institutions nearby.

MANAGING TECHNOLOGY

More and more schools and libraries have individuals or departments responsible for the technological infrastructure of the organization. However, Young Adult librarians and media specialists are still responsible for selecting software and sometimes audiovisual materials for their departments and often provide the content of the Young Adult Web page on the library's Web site.

Because of the familiarity of most teens with technology, it is important not to underestimate the importance of technology in the YA area. I would argue that the Young Adult Web page should be the most appealing, dynamic, and technologically sophisticated page on the library's Web site (simply because the teens who will be accessing it are likely to be some of your library's most technologically savvy patrons). It should include interactive elements, such as chat, e-mail, instant messaging (IM), and streaming video, and also have an eye-catching and attractive layout that is easy to navigate. It should move beyond book reviews and descriptions of library programs to provide online reference and readers advisory services as well as database access to content useful for last-minute report research. After-hours access is also important for teenagers who have very busy schedules (and a tendency to procrastinate).

For the same reasons, Young Adult departments should be the pioneers in their library in offering new software and devices (such as e-books, books on CD, gameboys, and DVDs) for circulation. Librarians who are not technologically inclined really need to make an effort to keep up with the latest developments when working with young adults. Otherwise, teens will grow up thinking of libraries and school libraries as places that weren't able to meet their needs and expectations, and they will be more likely to turn elsewhere for information as adults.

Check out the Young Adult Library Services Association (YALSA) Web site at www.ala.org/yalsa/booklists/index.html for lists of recommended books, audiobooks, DVDs, and videos.

PROGRAMS AND EVENTS

Programs are often the "hook" to get YAs to darken the door of the public library or to think of their school library as a fun and interesting place. The most important things to remember when planning a program or event are to start early, stay organized, and pay attention to the details. I recommend creating a timeline of all of the steps that need to be accomplished in the planning of your program and using a software program like Microsoft Outlook or an old-fashioned paper agenda to post reminders for each step in the process.

The Topic

Ideas for program topics can come from a variety of sources, including the popular media (*Survivor* and *Who Wants to Be a Millionaire* have been used as YA program themes in recent years), discussions with other librarians (in real life or on electronic discussion lists), conference programs, surveys, Teen Advisory Boards, or individual YA patrons.

Regardless of the source of the idea, run it past some local teens to get feedback on whether they think the idea will be a success (generally, if you can find a group of teens who are interested in attending the program and are willing to bring their friends, you can assume that the topic has some YA appeal). I recommend involving Teen Advisory Groups in the preparation and planning of all YA programs. This ensures that the teen perspective is represented throughout the process and also provides kids with a vested interest in the success of the program.

The Author/Performer(s)

Once you've determined your topic, you will need to consider who will conduct the program. As librarians, we generally don't have too much

---

A few common mistakes when doing anything new:

Avoid going from idea into full-scale operation without testing the idea. Don't omit the pilot stage. If you do, and skip from the concept to the full scale, even tiny and easily correctable flaws will destroy the innovation.

But also don't go by what "everybody knows" instead of looking out the window. What everybody knows is usually 20 years out of date. In political campaigns, those who look so promising at the beginning and then fizzle out are usually the ones who go by what they believe everybody knows. They haven't tested it, and it turns out that "this was 20 years ago" (Drucker, 1990: 69).

trouble locating subject experts on any given topic. Popular authors and performers are sure bets, but don't overlook other "experts" in your community. Local artisans and craftspeople can demonstrate their crafts, business and trade professionals can share information about their ar-

---

Popular YA authors can usually be contacted for school or library appearances through their publishers. Some of the larger publishers have author visit information available on their Web sites. These include:

Children's Book Council
www.cbcbooks.org/html/aboutauthors.html
This site contains information on planning author visits, including tips on how to choose an author and publisher. It also contains biographical information about authors and illustrators and information about their books, a list of "75 Authors/Illustrators That Everyone Should Know," and links to author and illustrator homepages.

HarperCollins Author Appearances
www.harperchildrens.com/hch/parents/schoolvisits.asp
This site contains suggestions on planning an author visit, instructions on how to contact a HarperCollins author, and tips on publicity, preparation, and other details.

Scholastic Author Studies Kit
www2.scholastic.com/teachers/authorsandbooks/authors andbooks.jhtml

Sharyn November's Web Site (with links to author homepages)
www.sharyn.org/
Sharyn November is an editor with Firebird Books, an imprint of Penguin Putnam, Inc., and a strong advocate for young adults and Young Adult literature. Her personal Web site contains information on a wide variety of resources related to children's and Young Adult literature as well as links to many author homepages.

Simon & Schuster Author Visits
www.harperchildrens.com/hch/parents/schoolvisits.asp
This site provides information about scheduled promotional tours for Simon & Schuster's children's and YA authors as well as tips on presenting an author appearance and information about how to schedule a Simon & Schuster author. It also contains links to Simon & Schuster authors' personal Web sites and biographical sheets on many of their authors and illustrators.

eas of work and interest, and even specialty retail vendors (such as book-store and comic book store owners) can present programs on their area of specialty.

If you have a decent program budget, you can also consider nationally recognized authors, performers, and experts on the topic you're presenting. Not all programs require an outside speaker, of course. Many libraries have conducted successful YA programs (such as murder mysteries, sleepovers, and summer reading programs) using only the expertise of library staff and Teen Advisory Boards.

Speakers should be scheduled up to six months in advance (possible longer for very popular figures). The popularity of the topic and the popularity of the speaker are the two main elements that are likely to determine the success of your program, although other elements, such as the choice of date and time, will also influence turnout. Try to schedule a time that doesn't conflict with school events or other popular YA activities in your area.

CONTRACTS

Once you have contacted a speaker and she has verbally agreed to present a program at the library, you should ask her to sign a contract, agreeing to the terms you have outlined. If your presenter is giving the program on a pro bono basis, you might want to send a less formal letter of confirmation instead (in keeping with your library's policies and legal counsel). In either case, the following elements should be included:

- the date of the agreement
- the names of the school/library and the individual/association entering into the agreement
- the scope of the program
- the contact person for the program
- what materials will be provided
- the date, time, and location of the program
- who will be responsible for providing the facility, handouts, publicity, equipment, and refreshments
- any payment or honorarium the speaker will receive
- any expenses (such as food, lodging, travel) that will be reimbursed and in what amount
- the conditions under which the contract/agreement might be amended or terminated
- dated signatures of both parties

You should request a biographical statement and photo as well as a program description from the presenter to use for publicity purposes. You may want to request a resumé or vitae as well, to use in preparing your introduction. It is a good idea to touch base with the presenter periodically throughout the planning process to see if any questions, needs, or concerns have arisen. You should also contact the performer a week or so before the program to confirm he still plans to present. And finally, don't forget to send a thank-you note after the program (traditional, handwritten is best) to thank the presenter for his time and report on how participants enjoyed the program.

COMPENSATION

Most professional speakers/performers request a fee for presenting library programs, although some will negotiate on their price or donate their services to a public library or school. Libraries should plan on paying at least a modest honorarium to all program presenters. If this is not possible, a small gift (such as a mug engraved with the library or school insignia) should be offered as a token of appreciation for their time and generosity. Costs can also be kept down by collaborating with another local library or school to bring in an author or performer to do presentations in more than one location during his visit.

TRAVEL, LODGING, MEALS, AND OTHER BENEFITS

The school or library should reimburse presenters for any costs associated with presenting the program, including the cost of handouts or other materials that will be provided to participants, travel, meals, and lodging. Presenters who come from out of town should also be included in any other events that occur in conjunction with their program. If funds permit, library staff should take the speaker out for lunch or dinner on the day of her program or host a reception with drinks and snacks after the program to allow teens to mingle with the speaker(s). These expenses should be planned for in the library budget and should not come out of the librarian's pocket.

The Event

The day of the program should be visualized in as much detail as possible. When participants arrive, there should be a librarian on hand to greet them. Consider whether you will need name tags or a sign-in sheet. Determine how long the program will last and provide time for breaks (with refreshments) if needed. A library staff member should introduce the program and thank any sponsors such as the Friends of the Library, or a local restaurant, that may have provided funding or in-kind donations for the program. Library materials that relate to the program should be placed on display in the room, and participants should be encouraged to check them out after the program.

You should also have a fall-back program of some sort planned in the event of an accident or presenter no-show. This could include reading excerpts from books on the proposed topic or playing a tape or video of a previous program that the presenter conducted (you might be able to obtain this in advance from the presenter herself).

The Space

Make sure your space is appropriate to your event. A water-balloon fight or dog show would most likely take place outside. Crafts that involve cooking should take place in a room with a kitchen, and painting and other messy activities should occur in a space where it is easy to clean up spills.

Determine (with the presenter) whether participants in the program will sit on chairs or on the floor and whether space will need to be made available for audience participation or movement (such as dance). Be sure to have any necessary equipment available and test that it is functioning properly at least a week before the program (to allow time to fix or replace broken equipment, if necessary). Test again the day before or the day of the program to make sure everything is still in working order. Involve teens in decorating the program space, as appropriate to the topic.

The Staff

Determine what library staff, volunteers, and teens will be available to assist in the preparation, set up, and clean up of the program. There should be at least two adults on hand for every program—one to greet participants and introduce the speaker and the other to be available to run last-minute errands or address any problems that might arise. Someone (staff or teen) should also be responsible for accompanying the speaker until it is time for her to begin her presentation.

The Sales/Souvenirs

Determine in advance whether you will have items available for sale at the program, in accordance with your school or library policies. The most common items sold at library programs are books by presenting authors. However, your library or department should have a clear policy on sales

Marcia Posner offers the following guidelines when introducing a speaker:

1. If you are unacquainted with the speaker, take the time to talk to him before the meeting begins.
2. Set the stage with a few well-chosen, brief (or borrowed) remarks. Above all, be enthusiastic and alive.
3. Introduce the speaker as if you yourself were eager to hear him.
4. Take time to frame your introduction of the speaker so your presentation is not stereotyped. Remember these words, "why," "what," and "who."
   a. Why is the speaker present? Because of his unique qualifications and background. Explain just enough to create interested expectation.
   b. What is the theme? Speak the title clearly and distinctly.
   c. If possible, do not mention the speaker's name until the very last words are spoken to spare the speaker embarrassment. Be sure your pronunciation of the speaker's name is correct and distinctly spoken.
5. Be brutally brief—60 seconds tops for your introduction.
6. When making the transition from one speaker to the next (if you have more than one speaker), listen carefully for one good point upon which you can graciously comment. (1997: 296)

of promotional items and souvenirs that should be equitably enforced for all programs.

If you allow sales of books or other items, determine whether library staff will handle this activity (as they are often requested to do in the case of books that are sent directly from the publisher to promote a presenting author) or whether a local agency (such as a bookstore) will take responsibility for this task. It is easier if an outside agency is available to handle sales, but it can also be done successfully using library staff, provided there is some means of keeping track of money received, change given, and items sold (such as a cash register). Don't forget to charge sales tax if it applies.

Promotion

Perhaps even more important to the success of a program than the topic and the person presenting is how well it is advertised. Particularly when you are targeting an audience of busy teenagers, who have a myriad of school-related and extracurricular activities competing for their time, it is essential to publicize your programs and publicize them well.

How to Market YA Programs

If your library has a public relations department, rely on their skills to create slick, eye-catching posters, flyers and brochures, and well-phrased press releases to promote your program. If you are responsible for creating promotional materials yourself, make use of the technologies available to you. It is no longer acceptable to advertise programs with handwritten signs (with the possible exception of an artist's rendition). Make use of the talents of your teen patrons. At a library I used to work with, a member of our Teen Library Council designed all our summer reading promotional materials. If you have a budget to compensate artists, teen artists should also be paid from this fund. Regardless of whether the library pays for artwork, the artist should be credited somewhere on your promotional materials.

On the day of the program, there should be adequate signage throughout the library (and particularly close to the entrance) to indicate where the program is taking place. If your library allows, consider making an announcement over the library's intercom to introduce the event and invite patrons to participate.

Where to Advertise

In short, everywhere. It is nearly impossible to overpublicize a YA program (although I have heard stories of library flyers sent to the schools en masse winding up as a sort of makeshift carpeting in the halls of the local high school). Schools in general, however, are an excellent place to direct-market programs to teens. If you work in a public library, find out (through your local media specialists) whose permission you need to obtain to distribute program flyers in the classrooms, and cultivate a good relationship with that person. Sometimes schools will be more willing to distribute public library promotional materials if public librarians deliver the handouts, precounted, and place them in each teacher's mailbox; or if they come to the classrooms and distribute the materials themselves, in conjunction with a short presentation about the program. When advertising in the schools, make sure to approach all schools in your area (including private schools and homeschool groups) that serve students in your target age range.

Other good places to display publicity materials are in local teen hangouts such as sports venues, youth associations, cafes, arcades and Internet cafes, popular restaurants and snack bars, movie theaters, malls, and the public library! Don't forget to target organizations, clubs, associations, and stores that relate to the topic of the program and to send special invitations to teens who have attended other programs at the library and adults who work with teens in the community. Of course, don't neglect the traditional approach to publicizing your program through local newspapers, TV and radio stations (also target broadcasts and publications created by and for teens), and on the school or library's Web page.

In a 1976 article in *School Library Journal*, Marcia Posner suggested, "You will need at least three press releases: one to inform the public that the library is planning a particular program, the second to remind the public that the program will be presented one week hence, and the third to show what a marvelous time was had at the program. This last should have black and white pictures or glossies to accompany it" (Posner, 1997: 295). This advice still holds true. Make an effort to determine who your contacts should be with the local media, find out when their deadlines are, and send press releases directly to these people in the formats they prefer.

If you expect a large turnout, you might want to require preregistration for the program. This provides you with a good estimate of how many participants to expect, as well as a list of phone numbers to call the day before the event. These names can also be put on a mailing list to advertise other programs in the future.

Evaluation

Although evaluation is generally not the most enjoyable aspect of program management, it is nonetheless essential. Particularly when you are working with YAs (who may not be willing to tell you the whole truth about how they enjoyed the program), it is important to solicit (optionally anonymous) feedback about your topics and presenters. The easiest way to do this is through a brief, specific program evaluation form. Your form should contain no more than ten (and preferably more like five) questions about the program, with multiple-choice answers (such as a rating from 1 [poor] to 5 [excellent]) and a space for additional comments. The last question should invite participants to suggest additional program topics and presenters.

One way to insure that teens will complete program evaluations is to "bribe" them with a gift when they turn it in (consult with your teen library council, students, or regular teen patrons for ideas for inexpensive gifts with teen appeal—candy always works . . .). Or you could use the completed evaluations (if they aren't anonymous) as raffle tickets to give away larger door prizes (which might be donated from local stores).

After you collect the evaluations from program participants, compile the responses in some orderly fashion. (This could be as simple as counting the ratings for each question and noting any particular comments that came up more than once or good ideas that kids provided.) Based on these responses, and on your own observations and verbal feedback about the program, jot down a few notes about what worked, what didn't, how many people attended, and things you would do differently in the future. Do this relatively soon after conducting the program (at the same time you are writing a thank-you note to the performer is a good way to remember) so the impressions are still fresh in your mind.

These evaluations will help you to determine how to proceed when planning future programs, and they will also provide you with statistics and pithy comments to include in your department's annual report.

Managing the Young Adult collection and hosting special events are two of the most fun activities in Young Adult librarianship (next to working with the kids, of course). Whatever you do, don't get so caught up in the details that you can't enjoy the show!

REFERENCES

Drucker, Peter F. 1990. *Managing the Non-profit Organization.* New York: HarperCollins.

Posner, Marcia. 1997. "P.P. and P.R.: Two Keys to Circulation Success." In *School Library Journal's Best: A Reader for Children's, Young Adult, and School Librarians.* Edited by Lillian N. Gerhardt; compiled by Marilyn L. Miller and Thomas W. Downen. New York: Neal-Schuman.

Chapter 6

Managing Administrative Duties: Paperwork and Planning

PLANNING

Often librarians—especially YA librarians and media specialists, who are responsible for providing direct service to patrons as well as managing their department or media center—have trouble finding the time to plan. Without planning, there is no way to determine where you are going or how to tell when you have gotten there. Although Chapter 8 will offer strategies for making time for important tasks such as planning, this chapter will attempt to explain why planning is important and what type of planning it is important to do.

Luckily, there has been an explosion of planning documents available in the library field over the past few years. Some of the most useful to Young Adult librarians are *Planning for Results: A Public Library Transformation Process* by Ethel Himmel and William James Wilson (1998) and *Output Measures and More: Planning and Evaluating Public Library Services for Young Adults* by Virginia A. Walter (1995b). *Information Power* by the American Association of School Librarians (1998) can be a useful tool for school library media specialists.

Although *Planning for Results* is a tool designed for planning at the whole-library level, its strategies may be adapted to the Young Adult department or media center. (The first chapter of *Output Measures and More* provides examples of how to do this [Walter, 1995b: 8–21].) For example, in place of the library planning team, Young Adult planning should involve all YA or school media staff members; and in place of a community planning committee, young adults should be involved. It is essential to involve staff and teens in the planning of services for the same reasons it is important to involve YAs in program planning—the services will be more successful with staff and teen input, and staff and teens will have the incentive to support them.

Perhaps one of the reasons librarians are reluctant to embark on the planning process is that it seems so complex and cumbersome. Although there are many stages in comprehensive planning, it is also possible to adapt the planning process to the individual needs of your particular department. Some libraries will create mission statements, but not vision or values statements. Some will have a broad "Young Adult Services Plan" without more specific goals and objectives. Although the professional planners may frown on these less comprehensive approaches, I believe that some planning is better than no planning, and anything you can find the time to do will help.

The YA planning process should be conducted with the full acknowledgement and support of your library or school administration. In fact, planning and evaluation can be an excellent way to keep administrators informed about what goes on in your department and why your services are essential. This can be particularly important for school library media specialists, whose work is significantly different from the other teachers in the building (and quite possibly misunderstood by the principal).

DETERMINING STANDARDS OF SERVICE

The first step in planning is to gather information and assess how you are doing in meeting the needs of your target audience. This involves examining your current services as well as taking a look at the demographics of your community. You may feel your YA summer reading program has been successful since it attracts over 200 local teens. But if there are 2,000 teens enrolled in your middle and high schools, your summer reading program is serving only 10 percent of your target audience.

Sources of information about your department's services include:

- monthly reports
- circulation statistics
- program attendance and evaluations
- survey and focus group results
- media coverage
- anecdotal feedback from staff and patrons

Sources of demographic information include:

- census data (and local statistical publications such as the annual *Kids Count Data Book* for your state)
- school enrollment statistics (including the number of children in your community's school system who receive subsidized meals)
- geographic information system (GIS) data
- local or state planning documents

Remember that this process will be done for the purpose of planning only, so don't try to cover up any areas in which your services may fall short. No one outside of your department needs to know what you find out, unless you decide to share your data with administration in order to justify the need for additional funding to improve services.

ROLES AND SERVICE RESPONSES

Once you have collected information about your current services and community needs, involve staff and local teens in determining what roles your department should take on. These should follow from your library or school's priorities, but may have a unique slant. Virginia Walter has adapted the Public Library Association's "role priorities" to relate more directly to Young Adult services (1995a: 14–18). YALSA's competencies document (*Young Adults Deserve the Best*) may also be used as a benchmark for library services to young adults.

MISSION

"The library's mission statement tells the community what business the library is in. It says what the library does exceptionally well that is unique,

> The goal of the YA area of the Dallas Public Library is to provide for the informational, educational, recreational, and cultural needs of the teenagers of the city of Dallas by providing an attractive, comfortable, and functional facility; by selecting, acquiring, organizing, and making freely and easily accessible age-appropriate material in a variety of formats; through offering a variety of programs, services, and activities; and by making the Library's YA area an active, vital, and visible institution of the community.
>
> *Source:* Ray Sablack, YA/Teen Specialist for the City of Dallas Public Library System

> I know a lot of companies with impressive mission statements. But there is a real difference, all the difference in the world, in the effectiveness of a mission statement created by everyone in the organization and one written by a few top executives behind a mahogany wall.
>
> One of the fundamental problems in organizations, including families, is that people are not committed to the determinations of other people for their lives. They simply don't buy into them. (Covey, 1989: 142–143)

or different, from what other agencies and organizations do" (Himmel and Wilson, 1998: 31). The Young Adult mission statement should do the same for the YA department or school media center. As is the case with service responses and role priorities, the YA mission statement should follow from the library's or school's mission statement. Walter gives an example of how to adapt a library's mission statement to relate more specifically to young adults in *Output Measures and More* (1995b: 18), but you might want to create a separate statement that addresses the particular strengths of your department.

Many library and business planning resources provide detailed instructions on creating a mission statement. In short, it should be concise and quantitative. All YA staff should have input in its creation and should "buy in" to the message it conveys. Think of the mission statement as the "ultimate answer." Whenever you are at a crossroads and wondering which way to go in your department, your mission statement should provide you with direction.

VISION

"Unlike the mission statement, which says what the library's business is *now*, the vision statement tries to articulate what the world *will be* like when the mission is accomplished. It is value-laden, optimistic, and uplifting, designed to inspire people with enthusiasm for the organization and its business" (Walter, 1995a: 18). If the mission answers the question "What are we doing," the vision should answer the question "Where are we going?" and do it in the most inspiring manner possible. The vision statement doesn't need to be quite as concise as the mission statement, but it should be brief and relevant enough for staff and patrons to remember. It may also address issues outside of the direct library set-

The following vision statement was created by the teens of Tucson and Pima County (Arizona) and describes how youth would like their capacity for educational and career success to be strengthened over the next five years:

> To create a partnership of advocacy among youth, the library, and the community which will inspire youth creativity, strengthen youth leadership, and support self determination to secure a successful future in a safe, fun, educational, and enjoyable place. (*Teens & TTPL*, 1999: 6)

ting, such as social and economic conditions for young adults in the community.

VALUES

As individuals who work in libraries, we all bring our own personal values to the job. Often, those values are in keeping with the values we uphold at work. Sometimes, however, they conflict. For example, as a librarian, I uphold the principles of intellectual freedom and resist censorship. However, as a feminist, I object to YA skateboard magazines that portray women in a derogatory manner. As a Young Adult librarian, I had to work against my personal bias in providing materials I didn't personally approve of.

These types of contradictions occur in libraries all the time; and they should, if we are to meet the diverse needs of all the members of our community. The personal values of your staff members may conflict with

Affirming Shared Values
√ Get together to start drafting your group's credo.
√ Make sure there is agreement around values.
√ Conduct a values survey.
√ Connect values with reasons (whys).
√ Structure cooperative goals.
√ Make sure everybody knows the business.
√ Be an enthusiastic spokesperson for shared values.
√ Accumulate yesses (say, "yes, and . . ." instead of "yes, but . . .").
√ Go slow to go fast (take small steps).
√ Establish a sunset statute for your credo (reassess periodically).
(adapted from Kouzes and Posner, 1993: 145–152)

those of other staff members as well. But all YA staff members must agree to put aside their personal biases in favor of upholding a set of departmental values that protect the needs of YAs in the library.

Like other planning documents, YA value statements should follow from the school or library's values, if they have been articulated. They should also take into account the work values of all members of the Young Adult department or school media center staff. An excellent guide in determining group values is *Organizational Vision, Values and Mission: A Fifty Minute Series Book* by Cynthia D. Scott (1994). The American Library Association's Core Values Task Force has also drafted a statement of core values for the profession (available at www.ala.org/congress/corevalues/), which could serve as a resource or model in developing a Young Adult values statement.

GOALS AND OBJECTIVES

Goals are long-range (usually three- to five-year) plans that follow from your service responses and mission and vision statements. "Objectives are the specific, short-range, quantifiable results that the library plans to accomplish on its way to achieving its goals. For each goal, the library would typically develop two or three objectives. The goals will remain constant for several years; the objectives will usually be formulated every year, often in connection with the budget cycle" (Walter, 1995a: 19).

For example, if your needs assessment determined there was a high rate of teen pregnancy in your area, one of your long-range goals might be to educate teens about reproduction and contraception. Your objectives might include meeting with school and other health professionals to share resources, developing a health materials collection, and conducting outreach programs (in conjunction with other youth services agencies) to promote the collection.

COMMUNICATION AND IMPLEMENTATION

As stated earlier, staff and teens should be involved in every step of the planning process. After the initial planning sessions, managers bear the responsibility of keeping the departmental mission, vision, and values in the minds of staff and patrons. This begins with publicity and public relations—once you have developed these guiding statements and they have been approved by administration, post them on the wall in your department; publish them in the staff newsletter; talk about your planning process at library, school-wide, and community meetings; include them in promotional materials; and share them with the public.

Specific staff members should be identified to take responsibility for accomplishing each of the department's objectives (often with the help of others) and they should be held accountable for accomplishing these tasks. Progress reports should be given at staff meetings so the entire department can see the tangible results of the planning process. Achievement of goals should be celebrated and made known to library administration and the public.

POLICIES AND PROCEDURES

"Policy is the why of doing something—the clarification of a library's philosophy and mission. Procedures, on the other hand, are the practical guides that instruct the staff how to handle specific situations" (Wagner and Wronka, 1995: 47). For example, your library might have a policy that minors unaccompanied by an adult will not be left alone at the library after closing. Your procedures would spell out who will remain with the student, for how long, and who to contact if the parent or guardian is unavailable.

Library policies are generally determined on a building or system-wide level, ideally with input from members of each department, and ap-

---

Policy Development Checklist

This checklist may be useful in reviewing steps for developing policy statements:

❑ Develop library and youth services mission statements and roles statements in context of all library services.
❑ Review existing library policies in light of the mission and roles statements.
❑ Involve staff and board in identifying new policy needs.
❑ Conduct literature searches and examine sample policies.
❑ Draft policy. Review and revise after staff discussion.
❑ Finalize policy. Seek administrative approval, followed by board approval.
❑ Determine implementation timeline, resources needed, and individuals responsible for implementation.
❑ Identify and develop necessary procedures to implement policy.
❑ Inform library users of both policy and procedures.
❑ Develop process for periodic review and evaluation of policy and procedures. (Wagner and Wronka, 1995: 45)

proved by the library board. Although some procedures are also determined at the organizational level, individual departments generally have
more leeway in determining procedures that relate to the specific functions of that department. "Procedures can minutely prescribe staff behavior and do not require board actions, so they are much more easily
revised or modified than policy. They must be consistently applied but
must also be flexible enough to adapt to the everyday reality of library
life" (Wagner and Wronka, 1995: 47).

The Young Adult supervisor's responsibility is to make sure library
policies and procedures don't discriminate against teens (for example, a
policy that prohibits more than three people from sitting together con-
tradicts a young adult developmental need and may prohibit students
from collaborating on school assignments), and to ensure that policies
and procedures are being equitably enforced (and that teens aren't being unfairly targeted).

REPORTS AND STATISTICS

The planning process as described in this chapter begins and ends with
an examination of reports and statistics. It is imperative that accurate
records are kept. Since goals and objectives should be objectively quantifiable, reports and statistics are what will determine whether you have
met your goals. This data tells you where you are in relation to where
you have been. Accurate recordkeeping is also an excellent way to justify the need for additional funds and services.

Output Measures and More (1995b) provides many objective means
of measuring Young Adult services. Humanize your reports with some
subjective feedback as well. Use excerpts from program evaluations and
comments of staff and patrons to highlight the emotion behind the numbers.

One of the most effective planning tools I have encountered is a formal or informal monthly departmental report. Whether or not you are
required to compile such a report for your principal, library director, or
board, it is a good idea to do so. This is an excellent way to keep your
supervisors (and often the whole library, if such reports are included in
board meeting minutes) informed of what you have been doing. It also
provides month-by-month documentation of the steps you are taking to
achieve departmental goals.

The easiest way to compile a monthly report is chronologically. Include a brief description of meetings, programs, publications, and other
significant events. The report should also contain information about any
assigned tasks that were not accomplished, with an explanation of what

went wrong. (This type of documentation may help you justify additional staff or funding.) Monthly report descriptions should be as objective and measurable as possible and include attendance statistics for meetings and programs.

EVALUATION OF SERVICES

Virginia Walter states that the goal of evaluation is ". . . not to *prove* but to *improve.* Evaluation can provide you with information that will help you make better decisions and improve the programs and services you offer" (1995b: 52). Although reports and statistics can provide you with the hard data to show where your money is going and what kinds of services you are providing to your patrons, as well as how those services are used in comparison to other departments, the ultimate goal of evaluation is to measure yourself against your own past performance and to ensure that you are constantly responding to community needs and interests and continually improving your services.

In addition to individual and specific service evaluations, periodically do a more comprehensive evaluation of Young Adult (or school media) services in general, which could include surveys and focus groups to determine how your patrons feel about the services you currently offer, and also to find out what services your patrons would like you to offer that you don't already. Ideally, you should work with a professional consultant or a nearby university to develop a statistically significant survey, but you can also receive good anecdotal information with a less formal approach. Be sure to ask specific questions about current library services as well as provide ideas for services your library doesn't currently provide (and allow respondents to add to those ideas).

A comprehensive evaluation plan is both the final step of the planning process and the first step in beginning the process over again. Effective planning, like effective staff performance evaluation, is not a one-time deal, but an ongoing system.

REFERENCES

American Association of School Librarians. 1998. *Information Power: Building Partnerships for Learning.* Chicago: American Library Association.

Covey, Stephen R. 1989. *The 7 Habits of Highly Effective People: Restoring the Character Ethic.* New York: Simon & Schuster.

Himmel, Ethel, and William James Wilson. 1998. *Planning for Results:*

A *Public Library Transformation Process*. Chicago: American Library Association.

Kouzes, James M., and Barry Z. Posner. 1993. *Credibility: How Leaders Gain and Lose It, Why People Demand It*. San Francisco: Jossey-Bass.

Population Reference Bureau (PRB). *Kids Count Data Book 2000: State Profiles of Child Well-Being*. Baltimore, Md.: Annie E. Casey Foundation, KINETIK Communication Graphics, Inc.

Scott, Cynthia D., et al. 1994. *Organizational Vision, Values and Mission: A Fifty-Minute Series Book*. Menlo Park, Calif.: Crisp Publishers.

Teens & TPPL: A Plan for Youth Development. June 1999. Tucson, Ariz.: Tucson-Pima Public Library.

Wagner, Mary M., and Gretchen Wronka. 1995. "Youth Services Policies and Procedures." In *Youth Services Librarians as Managers: A How-To Guide from Budgeting to Personnel*. Edited by Kathleen Staerkel, Mary Fellows, and Sue McCleaf Nespeca. Chicago: American Library Association.

Walter, Virginia A. 1995a. "Evaluating Library Services and Programs." In *Youth Services Librarians as Managers: A How-To Guide from Budgeting to Personnel*. Edited by Kathleen Staerkel, Mary Fellows, and Sue McCleaf Nespeca. Chicago: American Library Association.

Walter, Virginia A. 1995b. *Output Measures and More: Planning and Evaluating Public Library Services for Young Adults*. Chicago: American Library Association.

Chapter 7

Managing the YA Budget

> To be meaningful, a budget or an annual plan must be based on a long-range action plan that looks at such issues as the firm's business, its priorities, its future direction and the resources needed to achieve its goals. (California Society of Certified Public Accountants, 1994: 18–19)

HOW TO CONVINCE ADMINISTRATION THAT YOU NEED MONEY

Some YA librarians are fortunate to have healthy Young Adult budgets. But the many who don't may need to convince administrators of the importance of providing Young Adult services. The good news is that once you have completed the planning process you have already gathered a lot of data that will help you justify funding for Young Adult services. It is mostly a matter of manipulating that data to prove there is a demand for the services you want to provide and that you will need more money to meet that demand.

Comparison Shopping

The easiest way to do this is to compare your statistics:

- Find out how many students are in the middle and high schools in your area and compare that number to the number of cardholders your library has between the ages of 12 and 18.
- Compare the number of YA cardholders at your library to the number of YA cardholders at other libraries in your area.
- If your library has the capability of determining the annual circulation on YA cards, compare that to the circulation on the cards of other age groups in the library.

- Compare the annual circulation on YA cards to the annual circulation of YA materials to determine how much YAs are using materials outside of the YA collection.
- Compare the circulation of materials in the Young Adult area to the circulation of materials in other departments in the library. (Be sure to factor in the size of each collection and do these comparisons as percentages.)
- Compare the circulation of materials to YAs (and the circulation of YA materials) to the circulation of materials to students at local schools and at other local libraries.
- Determine the amount spent per YA in your community on materials and programming by dividing the amount spent on those line items by the YA population in your area. Do it again using the number of YA cardholders in place of the entire YA population.
- Compare the amount spent per YA to the amount spent per child in your library.
- Compare the number of (and attendance at) YA programs to children's (and adult) programs.
- Compare the percentage of YA patrons to the percentage of materials and programs offered for them.
- . . . and so on.

School librarians don't have other, similar departments to compare themselves to, but they can make similar comparisons with other school libraries in the area and with the public library. Use comparisons that turn up in your favor as examples of where you're already doing a good job. Use negative comparisons to justify why you need more funding to provide equitable service. "If, for instance, important determining factors in departmental budget allocations were the population served and the circulation, and youth services accounted for 30 percent of the population and 50 percent of the circulation, one would expect the department to receive at least 30 percent of the total public service department budget" (Deerr, 1995: 12).

Keeping Things in Perspective

Although you want to make a strong case for increased funding to your school or library administration, you must also be realistic and accept that administrators often have priorities other than guaranteeing the best possible service to young adults. It is also important to be aware that increases in the YA budget might mean decreases in other departments' budgets. Keep your colleagues informed about your financial planning and encourage them to do the same in their departments. Perhaps the YA budget will need to be raised incrementally over several years in order to eventually reach parity with other departments.

Also, consider the timing of your request against major library projects. "It can save you a lot of work and time if you know what the broad budgetary picture will be. If this is the year the administration is trying to obtain sizable raises for the staff or if benefits premiums just tripled, this is probably not the year to propose significant increases in other areas" (Deerr, 1995: 17).

It may be difficult to be patient; but in the long run, it will serve the YA department to be in good standing with other departments and library administration as well as to have a healthy budget.

Outside Sources of Funding

After you have made your budget request and have received a response from administration, you may find that you still don't have sufficient funds to accomplish all your goals. If that is the case, request permission from administration to explore outside sources of funding for your budget.

Programs are probably the easiest (and most common) item in the budget to subsidize with outside funding. You can draw on the needs identified in your planning process to obtain grants from local or national agencies that address some of the issues YAs are facing in your community. (There is often grant money available for projects that seek to reduce violence or tobacco use in teens or to improve self-esteem, for example.) You can also solicit cash or in-kind donations from local corporations and small retail stores. And don't underestimate the importance of individual donations. The vast majority of charitable dollars given in the private sector are from individuals rather than foundations and corporations (Rosenzweig, 1989: 71).

Also, don't overlook sources close to home. Many libraries subsidize programs with funding from the Friends of the Library or Library Foundation. The Parent Teacher Organization (or some variation thereof) might be a resource for school media center funding, and don't forget patrons and their parents. Although most school and public libraries offer their programs and services for free, students and Teen Advisory Board members can be involved in campaign drives to raise money for YA and school library services (as they often do for school field trips and extracurricular activities).

It should be noted that fundraising should be viewed as a stopgap measure—to get you by until adequate funds are made available in the library budget to support Young Adult services and programs. Funds from outside sources should not be viewed as a viable alternative to library funding for essential services.

WHAT TO DO WITH THE MONEY YOU GET (FINANCIAL PLANNING)

"Once the strategic plan timetable is in place, it becomes the basis for the annual plan, also called the budget" (California Society of Certified Public Accountants, 1994: 18,19). Your priorities for spending should follow directly from the needs you determined in your needs assessment and the goals and objectives you developed to meet those needs in the planning process.

HOW TO KEEP TRACK OF THE MONEY YOU HAVE

In a survey of 60 libraries in Bergen County, New Jersey, Judah Hamer determined that only 66 percent of the surveyed libraries were able to state how much they spent on YA materials ($4,937 on average). Nearly half did not have a programming line in their budget (Hamer, 2000). Although I am not aware of any statistically significant national data on this topic, I would venture to guess that this is pretty typical for libraries across the United States.

> Just imagine shopping for your weekly supply of food but having no idea how much money you have to spend. You might fill up your shopping cart with everything needed for the week, and when you get to the checkout, place the items on the counter in no particular order. The cashier starts to ring up the items and about halfway through informs you that you are out of funds. You return home with oatmeal, cookies, macaroni, fruit, and dishwashing detergent. Not exactly the ingredients of a well-stocked kitchen!
>
> While this scenario may seem absurd, it is unfortunately not that different from the way in which many youth services librarians are expected (or choose) to run their libraries or departments. Just as the shopper was unable to attain a goal of providing a week's worth of well-balanced nutritional food, librarians cannot possibly meet the goals of their public library or school without a budget. (Deerr, 1995: 11)

If your library has a budget team, offer to serve on it. If it does not (or if your offer is refused), submit a YA budget anyway. If it is not approved, still keep track of your spending in the following areas (at minimum), so you can do informal, financial planning on the department level, at the very least:

Personnel
Professional Development
Collection
Programs
Supplies

Developing a Library Budget

Kathleen Deerr gives a good overview of types of budgets appropriate for libraries in her chapter on "Budgeting" in *Youth Services Librarians as Managers: A How-To Guide from Budgeting to Personnel* (1995: 11–21). The easiest and by far most common system is line-item budgeting. In this system, each category of spending is listed as a separate item, with subcategories to keep track of spending in particular areas (for example, books, audiotapes, videos, and CD-ROMs might be subcategories under the category for YA Collection). The current year's budget is generally based on the previous year's budget, with accommodations made for any special circumstances. (If you have just completed Young Adult Services planning or assessment for the first time, those circumstances may affect a significant increase in the YA budget from one year to the next.) An explanation is generally provided for any significant difference in a department or line-item budget from year to year.

If you are presenting a budget to your administration for approval, I recommend accompanying it with a narrative that describes, in plain English, why you need the funding you have requested (in addition to the notes in the budget itself that explain increases in individual line items). Accompanying your request with anecdotes about your department's services and quotations from patrons and their parents can help tie your department's budget to the eventual impact that your library services have on the community, which may help persuade administrators to approve funding increases.

Developing a Budget for Outside Sources of Funding

If the Friends of the Library or another benefactor funds several YA programs over the course of the year, present that group with an annual budget, which anticipates all the programs you will request funding for and the amounts you will need for each program (rather than approach them several times throughout the year as needs arise). This will demonstrate that you have given thoughtful consideration to how their money should be spent. You should do everything in your power to receive all the money up front, so you can adjust funds between line items if needed (for example, if you spend more than you anticipated on a performer for a program but less than you anticipated on handouts and other materials). Save all your receipts and include them with a report to the funding organization at the end of the year that shows how you spent their money, and don't forget to thank them for their generosity.

Although your proposal to a funding agency should broadly specify how the money will be spent, make sure the library retains the right to decide on specific materials and services. For example, if you receive a grant for teen health issues, you may specify in your proposal that a certain amount of funds will be put towards a teen health book collection. The funding organization should hold you accountable for spending the money on this type of collection; however, they should not have decision-making authority over what specific titles are purchased (that should be determined by your collection development policy).

Reimbursement

Many libraries routinely ask their staff members to pay for program materials, travel or lodging costs for professional development activities, or other expenses out of their own pocket, to be reimbursed later by the library. This translates to the staff member providing the library with an interest-free loan. During the weeks or months that it takes to process the reimbursement claim, the individual's money is not earning the interest or dividends it would in a savings or investment plan. This is not fair and should not be tolerated.

Libraries can apply for institutional credit cards that can be used to cover these types of expenses, or cash can be forwarded to staff members from the library's budget to cover anticipated work-related expenses. In the case of a cash advance, individuals will likely have to complete a form anticipating the amount they will need to cover their expenses and to follow up with a report (and accompanying receipts) to prove how the money was spent. Any surplus money not returned can be taken out of the employee's next paycheck.

Even though Young Adult and school librarians generally do not set the policy on reimbursement in their libraries, they can lobby on behalf of their staff for a fair method of paying for library expenses.

Keep Your Own Records

Whether your library has an accountant or the county handles the library budget, keep track of your own department's spending. Software products such as Quicken or QuickBooks make it easy to keep track of business expenses, but a simple database program such as Excel can also be used. In addition to helping you catch errors, keeping your own records will allow you to track types of spending your library does not. (For example, you may want to know how much you are spending on YA romance novels, but the library budget may group them under YA paperbacks.)

HOW TO MAKE SURE YOU'RE SPENDING YOUR MONEY WISELY

Thomas Stanley and William Danko, authors of *The Millionaire Next Door*, found in their analysis of some of the wealthiest Americans that the more time people spent on financial planning, the less they worried about their financial futures (1996: 73,95). The same goes for libraries. Good planning will go a long way to insure good spending. However, there are some objective ways of determining whether you're spending your money wisely.

Test Ideas

Before embarking on a new project or service, gather information from other libraries that have done something similar. Talk to your Teen Advisory Board or host a focus group to see if the idea has YA appeal. In some cases it might make sense to start small. Sometimes offering a pilot project of a program is a good way to determine whether it will be successful on a larger scale. However, a huge turnout to a pilot program is a better indicator that a large-scale program will be successful than a small turnout to a pilot program is an indicator that a larger program would not work. Sometimes, an idea that will fly with lots of youth and staff participation and marketing will not take off without the accompanying fanfare.

Evaluate

Attendance at programs, circulation of the Young Adult collection, and feedback on evaluation forms are all indicators of the success of YA programs and services. It can also be helpful to engage community residents (both library users and nonusers) in discussions about Young Adult services and listen closely to their input. Responsive programming and planning will win you support from the community should your budget ever be threatened. Taking evaluation data into consideration will affect program planning and collection development, which will in turn affect budget allocations and begin the whole cycle again.

REFERENCES

California Society of Certified Public Accountants. 1994. "Budget: A Tool for Navigating Your Business." *Outlook* 62, no. 2 (Summer): 18–21.

Deerr, Kathleen. 1995. "Budgeting." In *Youth Services Librarians as Managers: A How-To Guide from Budgeting to Personnel*. Edited by Kathleen Staerkel, Mary Fellows, and Sue McCleaf Nespeca. Chicago: American Library Association.

Hamer, Judah. "RE: YA Programming Budgets." PUBYAC listserv. www.pallasinc.com/pubyac (22 December 2000).

Rosenzweig, Susan. 1989. "Part I: Funding for Youth Services—How to Do It and Where to Find It." In *Managers and Missionaries: Library Services to Children and Young Adults in the Information Age*. Edited by Leslie Edmonds. Urbana-Champaign: University of Illinois Graduate School of Library and Information Science.

Stanley, Thomas J., and William D. Danko. 1996. *The Millionaire Next Door: The Surprising Secrets of America's Wealthy*. Atlanta: Longstreet Press.

Chapter 8

Managing Time
and Getting Organized

We often talk about "making time" or "managing time" as if we actually had any control over the amount of time we have. In reality, "Time is neutral, and the amount of time we have is non-negotiable. Everyone, from the CEO to the night janitor, is allotted the same 24 hours, the same 86,400 seconds, every day. So the key to our achievement isn't in how much time we have, but in how we use the time we have" (Preston, 1999: 13).

HOW ARE YOU SPENDING YOUR TIME?

If you're an average American adult, over a lifetime you'd spend approximately:

- five years waiting in line
- four years doing household chores
- three years in meetings
- six years waiting at red lights
- one year watching T.V. commercials

Although many of us feel that all we do is work, if you are like the average person, your attention is specifically focused on work-related tasks for only about 30 hours a week, and you spend approximately 10 or more hours a week doing things irrelevant to your job while you're at work, such as daydreaming or talking with your coworkers about non-job-related things. (Levey and Levey, 1998: 48)

Most of us who feel we don't have enough time to get the important things done at work are probably spending a good deal of our time on activities that are less important. We spend most of our time doing things that are urgent, but not necessarily important, whereas to be truly effective, we need to shift more attention to activities that are important but not necessarily urgent.

David Preston recommends creating a Time Investment Portfolio (TIP)© by evaluating how many hours per week you are devoting to each activity (Preston, 1999: 18). One easy way to do this is to wear an alarm watch set to go off every 30 minutes and carry a small notebook to jot down your activities. Or, if you are more disciplined, you might simply write down how much time you spend on each activity you do in the course of your day as you complete it. Don't leave your log until the end of the day, however, since it is nearly impossible to recall with any accuracy where your time really went. At the end of a week (or a month if you are really committed to seeing where your time goes), review your log. You might be surprised to see how much time you spend on time-filler.

This can be a good experiment to do with your staff members as well—to help them determine how they use their time and to encourage them to spend more time on their most important job responsibilities. "Matching the dominant time allocation of an individual with the key responsibilities of his/her position is extremely important" (Preston, 1999: 18).

HOW SHOULD YOU BE SPENDING YOUR TIME?

We are what we repeatedly do. Excellence, then, is not an act, but a habit. (attributed to Aristotle in Covey, 1989: 46)

The goals and objectives you developed during the planning process should serve as your priorities in day-to-day time management. If your objectives are specific enough, they should provide you with tasks to accomplish and deadlines to meet throughout the year. Monthly and weekly planning should follow from these objectives in order to meet your departmental goals. Stephen Covey recommends further organizing your time around the roles you play in your organization (and in your life) (1989: 164–168). For example, if you are responsible for staff supervision, collection development, and maintaining the YA page of the library's Web site, you should plan on setting aside a certain amount of time each week to work toward accomplishing goals in each of those areas.

For tips on using Microsoft Outlook in libraries, check out *Using Microsoft Outlook 2000; A How-To-Do-It Manual for Librarians* by Michael Sauers (Neal-Schuman, 2001).

"You already know from basic physics traveling north at high speed is useless if you want to go west. The same applies to time management. You must have a specific destination before efficiency pays off. Thus, planning is the most important part of time management" (Kaye, 1999: 19). The trouble is that most of us don't know how to make time to plan our time.

I suggest the following: Set aside one day per month for planning. (It could be the first day of the month, or the last day of the month, or your birthday; but make it the same day every month so that it's easy to remember.) If you don't think you can spare a whole day each month, consider devoting four hours per month to planning. This can be done in one half-day or in snatches of one hour per week.

During your planning time, review your department's mission, vision, goals, and objectives. Determine your own professional roles and regular responsibilities. Decide how much time per month, week, or day you are willing to devote to each task. Then work backward from deadlines, dividing your time among your priorities, remembering to include important, but less urgent tasks as well as the most urgent activities. You can use a traditional daily or weekly planner book to map out your time, or rely on a time management software program such as Microsoft Outlook.

TIME MANAGEMENT

To every thing there is a season, and a time to every purpose under the heaven. (Ecclesiastes 3:1)

Weekly Planning

Each week, prioritize your activities and create a "to do" list that focuses on each of your primary roles and responsibilities and also makes concrete progress towards long-term goals and objectives. Don't forget to set aside time for activities such as reading and learning. You may need to block out a specific time each day (or week) for these activities and force yourself to stick with it in order to avoid having these important tasks edged out by interruptions and unplanned distractions.

Stick to the amount of time you allocate for each task. This may require beginning projects farther in advance than you are accustomed to, but it is better to make slow but steady progress on a variety of tasks than to have to scramble to complete a task at the last minute. You may not achieve the same adrenaline rush that you do when you devote all your time to one project for an intense and frantic period, but the long-term benefits to your department—and your sanity—will be worth it.

"To Do" Lists

Most accomplished people are listmakers. "To do" lists serve several functions. They help you keep track of what needs to be done, and they help organize and prioritize those activities. I keep a fairly elaborate "to do" list on Microsoft Outlook. It allows me to list EVERY activity that needs to be done (from watering my garden to preparing a quarterly financial report) and to group those activities by category or date due. I like this system because it keeps the list of everything I need to do in one place, but also allows me to filter by category to look at only those tasks that need to be done for one project or those tasks that absolutely have to be done today, which keeps me from feeling too overwhelmed.

Whenever I think of something that needs to be done, I put it on the "to do" list, immediately. This insures that the task will get done, but doesn't pull me away from the current activity to do it. If the "to do" task has a hard-and-fast due date, I will mark that as well. I set aside time each week to examine each category on my "to do" list, so that I continue to make steady progress in all areas.

I sometimes use what I refer to as the "ten-minute rule" when creating my "to do" list. If a task will take less than ten minutes to accomplish, I will try to do it immediately, instead of writing it down on the "to do" list. This gives me the feeling of having accomplished a number of small tasks throughout the day, as well as keeping my "to do" list from getting cluttered up with minor things.

I also use the "to do" list as a reminder for long-range planning. At the end of a staff evaluation, for example, I might write the date of that employee's next performance evaluation on my calendar, and then make a note on my "to do" list to start preparing for the next evaluation a few weeks before the date of the appointment.

Time management consists of 2 steps: 1) Make a list of things to do and 2) Do the most important things first. Your choices will be based on your mission, goals and principles. (Kaye, 1999: 19)

Figure 8–1
Simple Systems for Dealing with Procrastination

- Start with the easiest or smallest part of the project first. Once started, momentum will carry you through to complete it.
- Make a list of all the tasks related to the project. This activity is easy and serves as the first step in starting most projects. Then select the most appealing task from the list.
- Schedule the work. Break the task into small assignments and schedule them on your calendar. Then, apply discipline to work through the schedule.
- Set a deadline for completing the task, even if it is an artificial one. Then work toward that deadline.
- Delegate the task. If you feel resistance to working on something, that may suggest others are better suited for it.
- Just jump in and start anywhere. Throwing yourself into a task may be the trick that starts you working on it.
- Promise yourself a reward when you finish. That may encourage you to start.
- Reevaluate the importance of the task. If it's unimportant, then forget it. Realize the key to accomplishing more is avoiding trivial tasks.

Kaye, Seve. (www.stevekaye.com) 1999. "How You Can Increase Your Productivity (Time Management Ideas)." *American Salesman* 44:5 (May).

WORKING FROM A "TO DO" LIST

At the beginning of each week, I look at my "to do" list to see what deadlines are approaching. Then I adjust the list so an approximately equal number of tasks are due each day (or, perhaps more accurately, so I will be spending approximately an equal amount of time each day on tasks with deadlines). Tasks with specific deadlines serve as my first priorities. Once I complete those, I devote some time daily to the tasks that don't have deadlines in each category of my list. In this way, I rotate through each category on my "to do" list so no one category gets neglected at the expense of the others. I try to set aside a certain number of hours each week to devote to each category on my "to do" list, and then stick to that amount. If I fall behind in one area, I make it up the following week. If I am chronically behind in a particular category, that may indicate the category really doesn't deserve the level of priority I've assigned to it. So I will address that issue during my next monthly planning session (and stick that on the "to do" list as well!).

Daily routine activities, such as checking mail, voice mail, and e-mail, don't have to go on the "to do" list, but they should be done at the same time every day, and these activities should be limited to a reasonable amount of time. (What each person considers to be a reasonable amount of time will vary, but if these types of maintenance tasks are interfering with accomplishing more important goals, that's a good sign you are spending too much time on them.)

Appointments and Errands

I do not recommend putting appointments (like meetings, classes, workshops, and other places you need to be at a particular time) on the "to do" list. As a rule of thumb, if there is a time associated with the activity, I mark it on my calendar, not the "to do" list.

Also, I have found it useful to list errands on a separate piece of paper (or in a separate file on a PDA*) so you can take the errands list with you when you leave the building and not have to sort through all your other activities to figure out what you're supposed to be doing. You can mark the time you plan to do errands on your agenda or calendar.

ORGANIZATIONAL TIPS TO SIMPLIFY YOUR LIFE

The secret to using your time efficiently is having an organized workspace. There are many books available with specific suggestions on how to organize offices, files, desks, drawers, and bookshelves to maximize efficiency. Each person needs to develop a system that works for her. However, here are some general guidelines to get you started:

- Make sure things you use every day (such as paper, pens, envelopes, staplers, your agenda or calendar, the computer printer) are within easy reach of your regular workspace.
- Keep files in a logical order, alphabetical or by category.
- Keep files you don't use every day out of sight in a file cabinet.
- Keep a space on your desk (a tray or letter holder) for items that require action within the next week
- File everything else, with the possible exception of things that are awaiting action from someone else. Those can be put in another file or letter holder (and make a note in your "to do" list to follow up if a response isn't received in a reasonable amount of time).

---

*A Personal Digital Assistant (PDA) is a handheld computer that allows you to easily carry electronic files you use on a regular basis (such as an agenda, "to do" list, or address book). Most PDAs have the capability of downloading books and some can also download music and provide Internet access.

- Open mail when it arrives and decide immediately whether is it is something you need or will use. If it's not, discard immediately. If it is something you need to take action on, place it in a file on your desk designated for that purpose. If it is something you don't need to act on but would like to have on hand to refer to later, file the document(s) in a filing cabinet. Using these simple steps can help avoid clutter, lost items, missed deadlines, and so on.
- Keep your workspace clear at all times.

REFERENCES

Covey, Stephen R. 1989. *The 7 Habits of Highly Effective People: Restoring the Character Ethic.* New York: Simon & Schuster.

Kaye, Steve. 1999. "How You Can Increase Your Productivity (Time Management Ideas)." *American Salesman* 44, no. 5 (May): 19–25.

Levey, Joel, and Michelle Levey. 1998. *Living in Balance: A Dynamic Approach for Creating Harmony & Wholeness in a Chaotic World.* Berkeley: Conari Press.

Preston, David R. 1999. "Time for Success: A New Approach to a Familiar Challenge." *American Salesman* 44, no. 5 (May): 13–18.

Sauers, Michael. 2001. *Microsoft Outlook 2000: A How-To-Do-It Manual for Librarians.* New York: Neal-Schuman.

Chapter 9

Managing Stress

Sometimes I go about with pity for myself and all the while Great Winds are carrying me across the sky.—Ojibway saying (Levey and Levey, 1998: 122)

Librarianship is a helping profession. More often than not, we put our patrons' needs ahead of our own. If we don't regularly take the time to replenish our physical and emotional reserves, we may find ourselves quickly burning out in a job we once loved. Some simple strategies can help us develop the strength, energy, and peace of mind that is required to effectively help others.

HOW TO AVOID STRESS IN THE FIRST PLACE

Surprisingly, the solution to stress is to begin to lower our tolerance to stress. This is the opposite of what most of us have been taught, but it is the truth. Lowering our tolerance to stress is based on the simple principle that our level of internal stress will always be exactly equal to our current tolerance. That is why people who can handle lots of stress always have to do just that. (Carlson, 1997: 105)

Most of us have come to accept stress as a necessary part of modern life. However, we all know people who seem to have managed to escape its effects. Those people stand out in our minds as peaceful, present, happy. We want to be like them, but we don't know how. We assume they were just lucky to be born with a laid-back personality type. Although people do begin to form emotional habits at a very young age, it is never too late to change.

Practicing stress-prevention techniques on a daily basis can help to improve our physical and emotional states so we are better able to address potentially stressful situations.

Meditation

One of the most useful stress reduction techniques is the practice of mindfulness (which will be discussed later in this chapter), and meditation is a great way to help develop that skill. There are many ways to meditate, which range from sitting quietly and watching your thoughts as they arise, to focusing on the breath or a word; generating positive thoughts and feelings towards yourself and others; repeating affirmations; conjuring specific, peaceful images; or imagining yourself in relaxing situations. There are books, audiotapes, and videos that describe these techniques in detail. Read the reviews or browse your library's collection until you find a system that appeals to you. Then try meditating for a certain amount of time every day. Give yourself some time to get used to it, and see for yourself whether it makes a difference in your level of stress and attitude toward work and life. Although some religions use meditation as a spiritual technique, there is nothing inherently religious about meditation and anyone can do it, regardless of her beliefs.

Exercise and Nutrition

Although Young Adult librarians often assist patrons by walking with them to show where items are located and may squat or climb when shelving books or creating displays and props for programs, librarianship is generally considered to be a sedentary job. We tend to do most of our work "in our heads" rather than with our bodies, so it's important that we take time to nurture our physical selves outside the library setting.

We all know eating right and exercising regularly will make us feel better physically, but studies have shown that exercise also has a positive effect on emotional states. It is as hard to find time to exercise as it is to do long-range planning, but both tasks are equally important. You won't achieve your work goals without first determining what they are and developing the steps to get there; and you won't be in top emotional shape for work unless you eat right and exercise your body. There's no way around it. You can work from dawn to dusk and you won't be as productive or successful (never mind happy and fulfilled) as you would be if you took breaks to eat well and exercise.

Some significant benefits of mindfulness include:

- improved focus, concentration, and precision
- enhanced quality of communication and relationships
- heightened clarity of your thinking and intentions
- improved efficiency and safety
- greater peace of mind and sense of flow
- mastery of stress
- insight and enhanced intuitive wisdom
- more authenticity, heart, soul, and caring in your life-work
- change resilience
- greater confidence, faith, and inner strength (Levey and Levey, 1998: 50)

Mindfulness

Nearly all the books and articles on stress reduction begin with the concept of mindfulness (whether or not they call it that). Mindfulness is simply being fully aware and present in the moment. Easier said than done.

Most of us have experienced moments of mindfulness (which are sometimes referred to as "flow") when we were so engrossed in an activity that time seemed to stand still and nothing else mattered but the task at hand. But, more often than not, we get distracted by expectations and deadlines and spend most of our time trying to do two (or more) things at once. It can't be done. Even when "multitasking" (which I don't recommend), your mind flits between one activity and the other, rather than focusing fully and completely on both.

The practice of mindfulness can also be helpful to identify the beginnings of stressful feelings. Unless we are fully aware and present in the moment, we may not even realize when we begin to show signs of stress (some typical warning signs are listed later in this chapter). Being mindful of our feelings can help us to identify when we are beginning feel stress, so we can examine those feelings and the situation that caused them rather than getting wrapped up in our own anxiety.

With a heart balanced by mindfulness, you can learn to:

- Examine your current situation;
- Examine your reaction patterns;
- Examine your options;
- Examine your ideal visions, goals, intentions, and desired outcomes; and
- Make the wisest decision for moving forward (Levey and Levey, 1998:123)

And finally, true mindfulness helps us keep our eye on the big picture. When we find ourselves getting caught up in the stressful details of our job, being fully mindful can help us see how this minor annoyance fits into the larger scheme of the goals we are trying to accomplish and, ultimately, the difference we hope to make in our lives.

ADDRESSING STRESSFUL FEELINGS

Through meditating regularly, eating well and exercising, practicing mindfulness, and fostering personal growth, we will be able to eliminate a good portion of our work (and personal) stress. However, there will be times when we slip into old habits, and what follows are some tips for dealing with some of the most common forms of stress for Young Adult librarians.

Coping with Change

> Those interested in perpetuating present conditions are always in tears about the marvelous past that is about to disappear, without having so much as a smile for the young future—Simone de Beauvoir (McDermott, 1992)

Because of rapid developments in information technology and the sheer volume of information in our current society, keeping up with continual change can be a huge source of stress for librarians.

Sandra Champion identifies the following symptoms of "Technostress" in her article by the same name (subtitled "Technology's Toll"):

Anxiety	Fear of losing autonomy
Denial	Fear of losing promotion opportunities
Resistance	Fear of losing control over work environment
Technophobia	Fear of social isolation
Panic	Fear of change
Conflict	Fear of loss of freedom, privacy, and control
Mental Fatigue	Fear that technology will increase literacy
Intolerance	Intimidation by documentation
Perfectionism	Fear of inability to keep up with rapid change
Physical Discomforts	Problems with relationships (1997: 239)

Think about change as a process similar to that which Elizabeth Kubler-Ross identified for adapting to loss. When faced with frequent change in the library, many staff members will respond with initial resistance, inspired by fear. This may be followed by a period of denial, which gradually transforms into acceptance once the new skills required for the change are mastered. Keeping this process in mind can help you deal with your own stress related to change, as well as help you learn to be more compassionate with the adaptation process of your staff members.

Though we may not have control over what types of changes and new technologies are introduced into our workplaces, we do have control over how we will respond to them. And trying to see the ultimate benefits of the change may help the adaptation process go more smoothly.

Interacting with Others

In his book *Emotional Intelligence*, Daniel Goleman describes the social and emotional (as opposed to intellectual) skills it takes to succeed in work and life situations. His definition of emotional intelligence is based on the work of Howard Gardner and Peter Salovey and contains the following components:

1. knowing one's emotions—self-awareness or mindfulness
2. managing emotions—recognizing feelings for what they are and dealing with them appropriately
3. motivating oneself—emotional self-control to achieve an ultimate goal
4. recognizing emotions in others—empathy
5. handling relationships—interacting skillfully with others (1995: 43)

As mentioned in Chapter 1, "people skills" are your most important management tool, and knowing how to "play well with others" can also prevent a great deal of stress. Most of the strategies in this book are designed to help develop these skills.

Play

The brain is a wonderful organ. It starts working the moment you get up in the morning and does not stop until you get to the office—Robert Frost (Hemsath and Yerkes, 1997: 6)

A series of business training books and videos is based on the management philosophy at the Pike Place Market Fish Company in Seattle. Anyone who has visited this open-air market has seen these fish throwers in action—singing, joking with customers, posing for photos, and, of course, throwing fish! Passersby gather to watch the employees, who are clearly having so much fun at their jobs.

Does this sound like your library or media center? Granted, we don't have any fish to throw (and it could be dangerous to throw books or other media), but having fun at work can be a great way to keep stress at bay. Working with young adults makes it easy to have fun! I have often said that managing adults is just like managing teens, except that adults don't have as good a sense of humor. The Teen Advisory Board at the Bloomington, Indiana, Public Library uses a rubber chicken as a "talking stick" to indicate whose turn it is to speak at their meetings. Some school media specialists in Iowa interrupt classes (with the prior approval of teachers) with impromptu "poetry breaks" during which they burst into the room, read a poem aloud to the class, and make an equally speedy exit. Being able to be silly and to have fun at work are some of the greatest perks of working with teenagers. Don't pass up the opportunity!

WHAT TO DO WHEN IT ALL GETS TO BE TOO MUCH

Although a certain amount of stress is to be expected in our work (and personal) lives, chronic stress, anxiety or depression can be seriously debilitating conditions that require professional help.

In her article "A Teacher's Stress Survival Guide," Meg A. Bozzone lists the following warning signs of stress:

- racing heart
- persistent neck, jaw, shoulder, or back tension
- general irritability
- inability to concentrate or racing thoughts
- impulsive behavior
- nightmares or insomnia
- headaches
- fatigue
- indigestion, diarrhea, or constipation
- difficulty making decisions
- excessive worrying
- loss of or excessive appetite
- feelings of weakness or dizziness (1995: 56)

If you experience any combination of these symptoms regularly, consult a health-care professional.

REFERENCES

Bozzone, Meg A. 1995. "A Teacher's Stress Survival Guide." *Instructor* 104, no. 5 (Jan-Feb): 55–57.

Carlson, Richard. 1997. *You Can Be Happy No Matter What*. Revised ed. Novato, California: New World Library.

Champion, Sandra. 1997. "Technostress: Technology's Toll." In *School Library Journal's Best: A Reader for Children's, Young Adult, and School Librarians*. Edited by Lillian N. Gerhardt; compiled by Marilyn L. Miller and Thomas W. Downen. New York: Neal-Schuman.

Goleman, Daniel. 1995. *Emotional Intelligence*. New York: Bantam Books.

Hemsath, Dave, and Leslie Yerkes. 1997. *301 Ways to Have Fun at Work*. San Francisco: Berrett-Koehler Publishers.

Levey, Joel, and Michelle Levey. 1998. *Living in Balance: A Dynamic Approach for Creating Harmony & Wholeness in a Chaotic World*. Berkeley: Conari Press.

McDermott, Lynda C. 1992. *Caught in the Middle: How to Survive and Thrive in Today's Management Squeeze*. Englewood Cliffs, N.J.: Prentice-Hall.

Chapter 10

Managing Work and Life

Success at work depends on success at home and vice versa. Although we try to artificially divide our lives between the hours we spend at the library and the hours we spend at our house, we all know that one affects the other, sometimes more than we would like it to. That is one reason why YA librarians should advocate for workplace policies (such as comp or flex time) that enhance a work-life balance.

In *Living in Balance*, Joel and Michelle Levey state:

> Sustained success in balancing career and relationships is a creative and dynamic process. It requires at least three primary elements:
> 1) a high degree of personal honesty and self-awareness;
> 2) skill and willingness to communicate what is true for you to others; and
> 3) a willingness to creatively collaborate, explore possibilities, and reach mutually satisfactory compromises with others. (1998: 232)

All three of these skills will be useful in approaching the various strategies provided in this chapter.

VALUES AND PRIORITIES

The actor George Burns once said, "I'd rather be a failure at something I enjoy than a success at something I hate!" (Levey and Levey, 1998: 38). But unfortunately, for many of us it can be terrifying to attempt what we really want to do. What if we fail? Then we will be left with nothing—not even our dream! Of course, if we never try, we will certainly never achieve our goals either. What follows are a few suggestions about how to go about determining what really matters in your work and life and how to begin moving in the direction of your life goals.

How to Determine What's Important

The personal planning process mirrors the professional planning process in that the first step toward achieving a goal is defining the goal in the first place. In his book *The Path of Least Resistance*, Robert Fritz argues that most people go through life responding to circumstances around them rather than by using the creative process to choose their own direction (1989: 4–5, 66–67).

There are many tools available to help you determine your life goals and priorities. When I was a sophomore in high school, our English teacher gave us the assignment of writing our life philosophy (after reading Thoreau and Emerson). I believe that is the only assignment I remember from high school because it was the only assignment directly relevant to the rest of my life. Although my life philosophy has certainly changed since that time, the habit of thinking about what really matters to me has continued to help me create my own life direction.

You can try these activities to help you determine what's most important to you:

Ask yourself:

1. Are you happy living how you are living and doing what you are doing?
2. Is what you are doing adding to the confusion?
3. What are you doing to further peace and contentment in your own life and in the world?
4. How will you be remembered after you are gone—either in absence or in death? (Levey and Levey, 1998: 290)

Stephen Lundin and James Arnold build on this idea of using future memory to rank priorities by suggesting that you determine what is most important to you by imagining yourself as an 85-year-old looking back. "As I look back over 85 years, the things which now seem to be most important to me are . . . " (1997: n. pag.)

Phillip McGraw suggests determining your life direction through "An Exercise in Primary Choice" (which needs to be supported by secondary decisions in order to come to fruition):

Step 1. Make a list of everything you want, from now through the rest of your life.

Step 2. Reread your list to make sure it includes all of the major components you want in your life.

Step 3. Test each item on your list with this question: "If I could have that, would I take it?"

Step 4. Continue the process until you have chosen every item you truly want on your list. (1999: 180–181)

Once you've spent some time determining what really matters to you, these priorities can be formalized into a personal mission statement.

Creating a Personal Mission Statement

Writing or reviewing a mission statement changes you because it forces you to think through your priorities deeply, carefully, and to align your behavior with your beliefs—Steven Covey (1989: 129)

If you can't run a successful business (or library) without a mission statement, then it follows that you may not be able to have the most optimally fulfilling life without creating and living according to a personal mission statement. When my husband and I got married, the minister who married us suggested we create a mission statement for our marriage to clarify our expectations of each other and of the relationship.

James Kouzes and Barry Posner suggest using the five P's to help you create a statement of personal purpose:

- Proficiency is the special skill, task, expertise, or talent that we possess or desire to possess at a level of personal mastery.
- Product is the activity we perform using our special proficiency.
- People are those individuals we most want to serve or enjoy being with.
- Place is the setting in which we most enjoy exercising our special skill or talent.
- Purpose is the benefit or result of exercising that skill or talent. (1993: 87)

Once you have written your personal mission statement, print it out and hang it in a visible place so you will be reminded of it often. Set aside time to review and revise your mission on a regular basis. Like a business mission statement, your personal mission should be a living document that drives the direction of your life and work.

How to Achieve Your Life Goals

If one advances confidently in the direction of his dreams and endeavors to live the life which he has imagined, he will meet with a success unexpected in common hours—Henry David Thoreau (1962: 343)

Once you've determined your priorities and created your personal mission statement, it still may not be precisely clear how you are going to follow through on your life goals. However, just by clarifying them (in the process of prioritizing) and verbalizing them (in creating a personal mission statement), you have already taken the first two steps toward achieving your goals.

In the words of Steven Covey, "*All things are created twice.* There's a mental or first creation, and a physical or second creation to all things" (1989: 99). Shakti Gawain explores this concept in great detail in her bestselling *Creative Visualization*, which includes many exercises and activities on how to transform ideas into action (1982).

In his book *Life Strategies*, Phillip McGraw offers a seven-step system toward acquiring your goals. (Note that these strategies work equally well in the workplace as on a personal level.)

Step 1: Express your goal in terms of specific events or behaviors.
Step 2: Express your goal in terms that can be measured.
Step 3: Assign a timeline to your goal.
Step 4: Choose a goal you can control.
Step 5: Plan and program a strategy that will get you to your goal.
Step 6: Define your goal in terms of steps.
Step 7: Create accountability for your progress toward your goal. (1999: 255–263)

Once you have established a strategy for achieving a life goal, it is merely a matter of following through on that plan, which, admittedly, requires commitment, dedication, and often persistence and hard work. But in the words of Lynda McDermott, "Once you establish and act on goals that approximate your personal vision of a balanced world, you can win with each step of the way rather than be caught up in an ethereal pursuit of happiness as if it were an end state" (1992: 179).

BALANCE: WHERE TO DRAW THE LINE

I would not want any person to give his or her life to an organization. One gives one's very best efforts. (Drucker, 1990: 21)

It can be difficult for Young Adult librarians to balance their work and home lives when they are assigned other responsibilities in addition to those that focus on Young Adult services, or if they try to provide the best possible service to patrons by setting unrealistic goals for themselves that require far more time and energy than they expected to give. A helpful suggestion for those who feel overworked is to think about the amount of time it will take to accomplish a task, then double it, and allow yourself the longer length of time to finish the project. This may mean accomplishing fewer activities each year, but the quality of service will probably improve (as will the quality of your life).

I believe many librarians, particularly youth services librarians, also struggle with the balance between work and life because so many schools and libraries are underfunded. Young Adult librarians and media specialists often feel compelled to bring work home in order to get it done because there simply isn't enough time and staff to accomplish everything at the library. Although these librarians surely have the best of intentions, regularly doing library work on personal time only cheapens the value of library work (and probably also has a negative effect on librarians' personal lives). Perhaps it will take the work not getting done for administrators to realize that YA departments need more staff or funding.

It *is* possible, and even desirable, to bring parts of your personal self to your work. Although there are certainly times when it is appropriate to keep personal opinions separate from professional decisions (as when doing collection development), the most successful librarians *do* feel a personal investment in their work. Lundin and Arnold suggest viewing our jobs as being "directly related to our own personal success, rather than something we just punch-in for" (1997: n. pag.).

Furthermore, it is important that our most basic personal values are consistent with those we are required to uphold at work. McDermott offers suggestions about applying life values to the workplace in her exercise, "Finding Your Voice":

One way to begin to examine whether you've lost your voice and whether you practice your values is to answer these questions for yourself:

- What are the things you value most or consider most important in terms of your working environment?
- Do those conditions exist today in your current working environment, the organizational unit which you manage?
- What have you done to create a working environment that reflects your values?
- What are you doing to coach and influence your organization's culture in the direction of your values?
- If you do not believe your organization will alter its values to be more in alignment with yours, what are you doing about leaving the organization? (1992: 88)

Until we are able to achieve a healthy balance between work and our personal lives, and until we are able to reconcile our personal values with our work values, we won't be able to live lives of true integrity.

IS THERE LIFE BEYOND THE LIBRARY? MANAGING YOURSELF

Knowing others is intelligence.
Knowing yourself is true wisdom.
Mastering others is strength.
Mastering yourself is true power.—Tao Te Ching (Levey, 1998: 116)

In addition to being the manager of a Young Adult services department or school library media center, you are also the manager of your own life, and you should take that role at least as seriously as you take your job. It is up to you to determine what is most important to you and to spend your time accordingly. It is up to you to decide what kind of attitude you will adopt to respond to a variety of situations. And it is up to you to provide opportunities for yourself to learn and grow.

Phillip McGraw suggests that you periodically give your life manager (yourself) a performance evaluation:

Disregarding the fact that your life manager is you, do a results-based assessment that takes into account at least the following criteria:

1. Is your life manager keeping you safe and secure from foolish risks?
2. Is your life manager putting you in situations where you can utilize all of your skills and abilities?
3. Is your life manager creating opportunities for you to get what you really want in this life?

4. Is your life manager taking care of your health and well-being, physically, mentally, emotionally, and spiritually?
5. Is your life manager selecting and pursuing relationships in which you can be healthy and flourish?
6. Is your life manager requiring you to reach and stretch for those things that will keep you fresh and young and alive?
7. Is your life manager designing your day-to-day flow so that you enjoy some peace and tranquility?
8. Is your life manager arranging for some fun and recreation in your life?
9. Is your life manager structuring your world so that there is balance among those things you consider to be important? (1999: 169–170)

As the quote at the beginning of this section indicates, self-mastery flows from self-knowledge, and the best way to get to know yourself is by taking the time to do those things you really, truly enjoy. Julia Cameron, author of *The Artist's Way*, recommends that creative people treat themselves to an "artist's date" at least once a week, in which they do something silly, creative, or fun, just for the heck of it. She believes this "down time" fuels creativity (1992: 18–24). Steven Covey refers to the same concept as "sharpening the saw." He recommends reading, writing, and learning as ways to develop our leadership center. "The idea is that when we take time to draw on the leadership center of our lives, what life is ultimately about, it spreads like an umbrella over everything else. It renews us, it refreshes us, particularly if we recommit to it" (Covey, 1989: 294).

Too often, we feel like we don't have enough time for ourselves. But if we view our lives as being comparable to our jobs, not making time for ourselves is tantamount to neglecting our life responsibilities. And for those of us who work with teenagers, we truly do need to refresh ourselves with things we love in order to be able to bring that enthusiasm to our jobs and the kids we serve.

I recently had a discussion with a high school friend in which I wondered aloud why our teachers (unfortunately, I hardly even knew the school librarian) didn't reach out more to encourage our interests and support us through that difficult time of adolescence. My friend said they probably did the best they could, given the resources they had to draw on.

It is up to each one of us to determine our own resources and to provide ourselves with the intellectual, emotional, and spiritual tools we need to manage our own lives, so that we will have enough left over to share with those who need us. Being effective self-managers, and taking the time for things that matter most to us, will also help the kids and colleagues we work with learn to do the same. And most importantly, it will allow us to get the most out of our jobs, by giving the most of ourselves.

RESOURCES

Cameron, Julia. 1992. *The Artist's Way: A Spiritual Path to Higher Creativity*. New York: Putnam.

Covey, Stephen R. 1989. *The 7 Habits of Highly Effective People: Restoring the Character Ethic*. New York: Simon & Schuster.

Drucker, Peter F. 1990. *Managing the Non-profit Organization*. New York: HarperCollins.

Gawain, Shakti. 1982. *Creative Visualization*. New York: Bantam Doubleday Dell.

Kouzes, James M., and Barry Z. Posner. 1993. *Credibility: How Leaders Gain and Lose It, Why People Demand It*. San Francisco: Jossey-Bass.

Levey, Joel, and Michelle Levey. 1998. *Living in Balance: A Dynamic Approach for Creating Harmony & Wholeness in a Chaotic World*. Berkeley: Conari Press.

Lundin, Stephen C., and James K. Arnold. 1997. *Personal Accountability: Your Path to a Rewarding Work Life*. Minneapolis: Charthouse International Learning Corporation.

McDermott, Lynda C. 1992. *Caught in the Middle: How to Survive and Thrive in Today's Management Squeeze*. Englewood Cliffs, N.J.: Prentice-Hall.

McGraw, Phillip C. 1999. *Life Strategies: Doing What Works, Doing What Matters*. New York: Hyperion.

Roesch, Roberta. 1996. *The Working Woman's Guide to Managing Time: Take Charge of Your Job and Your Life While Taking Care of Yourself*. Englewood Cliffs, N.J.: Prentice Hall.

Thoreau, Henry David. 1962. *Walden and Other Writings*. New York: Bantam Books.

Conclusion

EASIER SAID THAN DONE

Throughout the course of writing this book, many friends and colleagues shared their management trials and tribulations with me, in the hopes that I would be able to provide them with the magic bullet that would solve all their problems. Although I have included strategies that can be applied to a variety of issues, the trick about management (and personnel management in particular) is that every situation is unique. Another challenge is that managers often don't have a lot of time to consider the problem and identify the most appropriate strategy before they need to respond to a crisis. And finally, it is not always apparent which strategy will work best with a particular employee, teen, colleague, or situation.

Management is, at heart, a process of trial and error. Often, when we anticipate problems, things go remarkably smoothly (perhaps as a result of good preparation). On the other hand, we are also sometimes blindsided by situations we didn't anticipate. All library managers have good days and bad days: days when they feel they are on top of the world and other days when they feel they can't do anything right.

It is normal to sometimes be at a loss as to how to handle a particular situation. I hope this book will provide you with some ideas you can try when you encounter that challenging situation. It is sometimes difficult not to get discouraged when you are dealing with the tough issues involved with Young Adult services (censorship, behavior problems, and personnel issues are a few that come to mind). But studies have shown that people who doubt their performance are likely to have performed better than they thought. Only the truly incompetent are consistently self-confident.

And in the end, there is often no one "right way" to handle library management situations. Several approaches may be equally appropriate to a particular situation, and it may take a few tries before you find the one that works best for you. That's okay. In fact, that's good. By experimenting with a variety of management strategies you will be modeling the problem-solving process to your staff, colleagues, and teens, and hopefully involving all of them in finding the best solutions!

Notes & Credits

Chapter 1:

page 9: Covey, Stephen R. 1989. *The 7 Habits of Highly Effective People,* © 1989 Stephen R. Covey. p. 78. Reprinted with permission from Franklin Covey Co., www.franklincovey.com

page 11: 2000. Gossip: A Career Management Tool. *Library Mosaics* 11, no. 4.

page 17: Brinkman, Rick and Rick Kirschner. 1994. *Dealing With People You Can't Stand: How to Bring Out the Best in People at Their Worst.* New York, San Francisco, Washington D.C.: McGraw-Hill, Inc.

Figure 1-1: Covey, Stephen R. 1989. *The 7 Habits of Highly Effective People,* © 1989 Stephen R. Covey. p. 78. Reprinted with permission from Franklin Covey Co., www.franklincovey.com

Figure 1-2: Kouzes, James M. and Barry Z. Posner. Copyright © 1993. *Credibility: How Leaders Gain and Lose It, Why People Demand It.* San Francisco: Jossey-Bass Inc.:14. Reprinted by permission of John Wiley & Sons, Inc.

Chapter 2:

page 24: Holmes, George. 1995. *Helping Teenagers Into Adulthood.* Westport, Conn.: Praeger.

Figure 2-1: Copyright © 1994, by Jane Nelsen, Ed.D. and Lynn Lott, M.A. All rights reserved. Reprinted with permission of Prima Publishing from the book *Positive Discipline for Teenagers*

page 31: Holmes, George. 1995. *Helping Teenagers Into Adulthood.* Westport, Conn.: Praeger.

page 38: Copyright © 1994, by Jane Nelsen, Ed.D. and Lynn Lott, M.A. All rights reserved. Reprinted with permission of Prima Publishing from the book *Positive Discipline for Teenagers.*

Figure 2-2: Tapscott, Don. 1998. *Growing Up Digital: The Rise of the Net Generation*. New York: McGraw-Hill: 211. Reproduced with permission of the McGraw-Hill Companies.

Chapter 3:

Figure 3-1: Adapted with permission from the Missoula (MT) Public Library "New Employee Orientation Timeline" 2000

Figure 3-2: Adapted with permission from the Missoula (MT) Public Library "New Employee Orientation Timeline" October, 1999

Figure 3-3: McDermott, Lynda C. 1992. *Caught in the Middle: How to Survive and Thrive in Today's Management Squeeze*. Englewood Cliffs, NJ: Prentice-Hall Inc: 101.

Figure 3-4: Arnold, James K., and Stephen C. Lundin. *Personal Accountability: Your Path to a Rewarding Work Life*. Minneapolis: ChartHouse International Learning Corporation.

Figure 3-5: Schwartz, Roger M. © 1994. *The Skilled Facilitator: Practical Wisdom for Developing Effective Groups*. San Francisco: Jossey-Bass Inc.:238. Reprinted by permission of Jossey-Bass a subsidiary of John Wiley & Sons, Inc.

Figure 3-6: Schwartz, Roger M. © 1994. *The Skilled Facilitator: Practical Wisdom for Developing Effective Groups*. San Francisco: Jossey-Bass Inc.:75. Reprinted by permission of Jossey-Bass a subsidiary of John Wiley & Sons, Inc.

Chapter 8:

Figure 8-1: Roesch, Roberta. 1996. *The Working Woman's Guide to Managing Time: Take Charge of Your Job and Your Life While Taking Care of Yourself*. Englewood Cliffs, NJ: Prentice Hall: 64.

Index

About the Author

RENÉE J. VAILLANCOURT is a freelance writer, editor, and library consultant. She earned her MSLS at the Catholic University of America where she received a U.S. Department of Education Title IIB Scholarship for Young Adult Services. She has served as the Youth Services Librarian at the Lincoln (Rhode Island) Public Library, the Access Center Librarian (serving people with disabilities) at the Boston Public Library, the Young Adult Services Coordinator at the Carmel Clay (Indiana) Public Library, and the Assistant Director at the Missoula (Montana) Public Library.

She is the author of *Bare Bones Young Adult Services* (American Library Association: 2000) and several articles and book chapters on serving children and young adults in libraries. She has been active in YALSA since 1992 and has served on the Quick Picks, Youth Participation, and Publications committees. As a Serving the Underserved trainer, she has conducted numerous workshops on Young Adult services across the United States. She is currently Feature Editor of *Public Libraries* magazine, the journal of the Public Library Association, and a consulting editor with ALA Editions.